Fit for Business English

Konversation

Robert Tilley

Compact Verlag

Bisher sind in dieser Reihe erschienen:

- Fit for Business English – Telefonieren
- Fit for Business English – Korrespondenz
- Fit for Business English – Verkaufsgespräche
- Fit for Business English – Präsentationen
- Fit for Business English – Geschäftsreisen
- Fit for Business English – Konversation
- Fit for Business English – Redewendungen

Weitere Titel sind in Vorbereitung.

Chefredaktion: Dr. Angela Sendlinger
Redaktion: Helga Aichele
Fachredaktion: Anthony Moore
Übersetzung: Marc Hillefeld
Produktion: Wolfram Friedrich
Gestaltung: Hendryk Sommer
Titelabbildung: IFA-Bilderteam
Umschlaggestaltung: Axel Ganguin

ISBN 978-3-8174-7771-5
7277711

Besuchen Sie uns im Internet: www.compactverlag.de

Vorwort

Englisch ist die länderübergreifende Sprache der Wirtschaft. Angesichts der zunehmenden Globalisierung der Märkte werden gute Englischkenntnisse immer wichtiger für den beruflichen Erfolg.

Die Reihe **Fit for Business English** ermöglicht dem Benutzer die zielgerechte Vorbereitung auf verschiedene Themenbereiche des modernen Wirtschaftsenglisch.

Der Band **Fit for Business English – Konversation** trainiert speziell die englischsprachige Berufskommunikation. Dabei wird gezeigt, wie man im Gespräch geschickt Kontakte aufbaut, sich und das Unternehmen überzeugend darstellt und auch auf internationaler Ebene sicher argumentiert und kommuniziert.

Dies geschieht anhand einer Story: Der Deutsche Peter Brückner wird von seiner Firma nach England versetzt. Um den nötigen Lernspaß zu garantieren, werden seine Erlebnisse in humorvoller Weise dargestellt.

Alle Dialoge sind praxisnah und sowohl in englischer Sprache als auch in der deutschen Übersetzung angegeben. Die Schlüsselbegriffe sind im Text farbig hervorgehoben.

Nach jedem Dialog folgen zur Überprüfung und Vertiefung des gelernten Wortschatzes kurze Übungen. Die Lösungen sind im Anhang zu finden.

Sprachpraktische und kulturelle Besonderheiten werden an gegebener Stelle angemerkt. Hierzu gehören Tipps zum korrekten Sprachgebrauch sowie landeskundliche Hinweise.

Verschiedene Symbole zu Beginn jedes Abschnitts erleichtern dem Benutzer den Zugriff auf die für ihn relevanten Passagen.

Am Ende jedes Kapitels werden alle wichtigen Vokabeln und Redewendungen nochmals angeführt.

Mit einem abschließenden Test im Anhang kann der Leser seinen Kenntnisstand überprüfen.

Inhalt

Here we go: kleine Einleitung am Anfang des Kapitels

Talk Talk Talk: praxisnahe Dialoge mit deutschen Übersetzungen, die wichtigsten Stichwörter sind farbig markiert

Train Yourself: abwechslungsreiche Übungen trainieren den gelernten Wortschatz

Background Information: Wissenswertes zu Business und Landeskunde

Do's and Dont's: Tipps zum korrekten Verhalten in Geschäftssituationen

False Friends: Hinweise auf mögliche sprachliche Fehler

Vocabulary: Vokabelliste mit dem Wortschatz des Kapitels

The Test: Im Abschlusstest zeigt es sich: Was haben Sie gelernt? Wo sind vielleicht noch Ihre Schwächen?

Ready to talk: Alles Wichtige zum Nachschlagen

Glossary: Zusammenfassung aller neuen Vokabeln

Solutions: Die Lösungen zu Übungen im Text und zum Abschlusstest

Story

Peter Brückner ist 30 Jahre alt. Nach seinem BWL-Studium wurde er als Assistent des Vertriebsleiters bei der internationalen Firma ERGO Ltd. beschäftigt. ERGO Ltd. ist ein innovatives Unternehmen und hat sich auf die Produktion von Zubehörteilen im IT-Bereich spezialisiert.
Um Peter Brückner auf eine spätere Führungsposition vorzubereiten, wird er in die Filiale nach London versetzt, um dort die Abläufe des internationalen Vertriebs kennen zu lernen. Wie viele andere Unternehmen, legt auch ERGO Ltd. großen Wert darauf, dass künftige Führungskräfte Auslandserfahrungen sammeln.

Dieser Band der Reihe **Fit for Business English** zeigt, wie Peter Brückner die Berufskommunikation in englischer Sprache perfekt meistert. Tatkräftige Unterstützung erhält er dabei von seinen Kollegen und neuen Geschäftsfreunden, die ihm jederzeit mit nützlichen Tipps zur Seite stehen und ihn auf die kulturellen und sprachlichen Feinheiten hinweisen. Dies sind:

- James Morgan, Managing Director, direkter Vorgesetzter von Peter
- Steve Blackman, Leiter der Verkaufsabteilung
- Melissa Walker, ehemalige Marketing Managerin bei Ergo
- Beryl Platt, Marketing-Assistentin
- Lucy Scott, Sekretärin und »gute Seele« des Büros
- Chip (Charles Collyer), Kurier
- Don Schering, Office Manager der New Yorker Niederlassung
- Archie Atherton-Smythe, Vertreter des »Royal Star Banking«-Unternehmens
- Amanda Locke, Fernsehproduzentin und -moderatorin.

Schon bald ist Peter Brückner mit den wichtigsten Redewendungen vertraut und weiß, wie man Geschäftskontakte aufbaut, das Unternehmen vorstellt, über Arbeitskonditionen spricht, auf Konferenzen überzeugt und internationale Beziehungen pflegt.

Trade fair contacts
Messekontakte

Here we go

Im fünften Band von »Fit for Business English«, musste Peter geschäftlich nach Amerika reisen. Dort ließen wir ihn in Gesellschaft seiner früheren Kollegin Melissa Walker, Archie Atherton-Smythe, einer neuen Geschäftsbekanntschaft und der amerikanischen Fernsehmoderatorin Amanda Locke während einer Pause im Winter Garden Theatre, New York, zurück. Vorher sah Melissa, wie Peter und Amanda zum Spaß Diamantringe bei Tiffany's betrachteten – und sie scheint daraus Schlüsse gezogen zu haben ...

Talk Talk Talk

(After the show)	(Nach der Vorstellung)
A-S. Well, I'm not really one for musicals, but I must say I enjoyed that one. I can actually hum one of the numbers ...	A-S. Na ja, Musicals sind nicht wirklich mein Ding, aber ich muss sagen, dieses hat mir gefallen. Ich kann sogar noch einen Song summen ...
P. Oh, Archie, please spare us that. I don't want to be rude, but ...	P. Oh, Archie, bitte ersparen Sie uns das. Ich will nicht unhöflich sein, aber ...
A-S. No offence, no offence. But it's your round. That means a nightcap before turning in. Where do you suggest, Amanda?	A-S. Nichts für ungut, nichts für ungut. Aber jetzt sind Sie an der Reihe. Das bedeutet – ein Schlummertrunk vor dem nach Hause gehen. Was schlagen Sie vor, Amanda?
AL. There's a friendly bar I know	AL. Ich kenne da eine nette Bar

just off Times Square. Follow me. Flag down that cab, Peter!

gleich beim Times Square. Folgen Sie mir! Winken Sie das Taxi heran, Peter!

Background Information

»Flag down« means literally to wave a flag at a taxi so that it slows down and stops for you. In Britain, you'll hear talk of »flag days«, when charitable organizations sell small flags to wear in the lapel in exchange for contributions. The United States has its flag day, too – on June 14, when many states commemorate the adoption of the official U.S. flag, the »Stars and Stripes«, in 1777.
The verb »to flag«, by the way, means to hang loose, like a flag on its pole on a windless day, or to become tired and lose energy or interest.

Train Yourself

Archie suggests to Peter and Amanda that they visit a bar and have a final drink before »turning in« – meaning before going home to sleep. There are several other expressions using »turn«. **Select the correct ones in the following sentences:**

1. My neighbour's dog suddenly turned __________ me with frightening ferocity.
2. The nightwatchmen caught the thief and turned him __________ __________ to the police.
3. Just look at those youngsters dance. The music really turns them __________.
4. The road outside the town was flooded and police were turning __________ the traffic.
5. A visit to the local slaughterhouse turned me __________ meat for ever.
6. We're very near the house now, take the next turn __________.
7. They turned __________ his application to join the police because of his bad eyesight.
8. Turn __________ the bed now, I'll turn __________ the light, and then let's get some sleep.

9. They turned ______ for the appointment very late.
10. The company turned ______ more than six million dollars in its first year.

And the possibilities: *turn up, turn off, turn back, turn down, turn up, turn on, turn back, turn in*

Talk Talk Talk

(The Rooster bar)	(Die Rooster Bar)
P. Well, this is a snug place, Amanda. Now what's it to be? And you, Archie?	P. Na, das ist ein gemütliches Plätzchen, Amanda. Nun, was darf es sein? Und Sie, Archie?
A. I'll have a … why, there's Troy Everett, the producer. Troy! Over here! Come and join us! Troy, I haven't seen you for ages. **I'd like you to meet** my two friends from London. They're businessmen, I'm afraid, but they're good-looking enough to take roles in your next movie. Boys! This is Troy Everett, the film producer. Troy, **let me introduce you to** Peter Brückner and Archie Atherton-Smythe.	A. Ich nehme ein … he, da ist Troy Everett, der Produzent. Troy! Hier herüber. Komm und leiste uns Gesellschaft! Troy, ich habe dich eine Ewigkeit nicht gesehen. **Ich möchte, dass du** meine zwei Freunde aus London **kennen lernst**. Sie sind leider Geschäftsleute, aber sie sehen gut genug aus, um in deinem nächsten Film mitzuspielen. Jungs! Das ist Troy Everett, der Filmproduzent. Troy, **lass mich dir** Peter Brückner und Archie Atherton-Smythe **vorstellen.**
P. **How do you do**, I'm honoured to meet you.	P. **Guten Tag**, es ist mir eine Ehre, Sie kennen zu lernen.
A-S. How do you do, **I'm delighted to meet you**. Used to be in movies myself. Do you remember »Moon	A-S. Guten Tag, **erfreut, Sie kennen zu lernen.** Ich habe selbst schon in Filmen mitgespielt.

over the Ganges«? I was the ambassador's butler. I was screen-tested for the role of ambassador, but Gielgud got it.

Erinnern Sie sich an »Moon over the Ganges«? Ich war der Butler des Botschafters. Von mir wurden sogar schon Probeaufnahmen für die Rolle des Botschafters gemacht, aber Gielgud bekam sie.

A. Sir John Gielgud?

A. Sir John Gielgud?

A-S. No, dear girl. Some yank called Frankie Gielgud. He could **manage** an English accent rather well, though.
Oh, I do apologise. I didn't mean to call him a yank – he was a dear American colleague.

A-S. Nein, meine Liebe. Ein Yankee namens Frankie Gielgud. Obwohl er den englischen Akzent ziemlich gut **hinbekommen** hat.
Oh, ich bitte um Verzeihung. Ich wollte ihn nicht als Yankee bezeichnen – er war ein netter amerikanischer Kollege.

TE. And what are you guys doing in New York?

TE. Und was macht ihr Jungs in New York?

P. Well, I'm here to **take a look at my company's operation**.

P. Nun ja, ich bin hier, um **einen Blick auf die Tätigkeiten meiner Firma zu werfen**.

A-S. And I'm here to **represent my company at** an international security trade fair.

A-S. Und ich bin hier, um **meine Firma** bei einer internationalen Sicherheitsmesse zu **vertreten**.

TE. Fascinating. Amanda, can't you get them on TV?

TE. Faszinierend. Amanda, kannst du sie nicht ins Fernsehen bringen?

A. I'm **bargaining** with Archie for a large **overdraft** at one of his client banks in exchange for a spot, but he **drives a hard bargain**.

A. Ich **verhandle** gerade mit Archie wegen einer hohen **Überziehungssumme** bei einer seiner Bankkunden im Austausch gegen einen Auftritt, aber er **führt harte Verhandlungen**.

Peter could get on just with his looks, but he's shy. He's German, you know.

Peter könnte das alleine mit seinem Aussehen schaffen, aber er ist schüchtern. Er ist Deutscher, weißt du.

TE. A Kraut? Well, will you get a load of that?

TE. Ein Kraut? So was, ist das zu fassen?

A-S. What are you drinking? Peter here is paying. **In return,** I am inviting him to the trade fair tomorrow.

A-S. Was trinken Sie? Peter hier zahlt. **Im Gegenzug** lade ich ihn morgen zur Fachmesse ein.

TE. Doesn't sound like much of a deal to me. Peter, if you fancy a visit to my studio, give me a call. **Here's my card.** Here's one for you, too, Archie. But I warn you – we don't make movies with English butlers any more ...

TE. Für mich hört sich das nach keinem guten Geschäft an. Peter, wenn Sie Lust auf einen Besuch in meinem Studio haben, rufen Sie mich an. **Hier ist meine Karte.** Hier ist auch eine für Sie, Archie. Aber ich warne Sie – wir machen keine Filme mehr mit englischen Butlern ...

Background Information

A point of etiquette

Don't be offended if, in informal conversation, you are called a Kraut. It's by no means intended as an **insult**. Troy Everett **possibly stepped out of line** by using the term within moments of meeting Peter – but he's in the movie business, after all. He probably took no exception to being called a yank by Archie. If we had stayed with the group a while longer we may have heard Archie being called a limey by Troy, and we would certainly have witnessed some friendly British-American rivalries being expressed. The term »limey«, by the way, has interesting origins: it stems from the former practice on British naval vessels of serving lime juice to sailors to boost their resistance to the dreaded disease scurvy, caused by a deficiency in vitamin C.

Train Yourself

Let's turn back ...

The word »turn« also forms the basis of several common expressions.

Find the ones to fit the gaps in the following sentences:

1. That was quite a party last night. Dave certainly knows how to ______.
2. Well, I found the music he played was a complete ______.
3. But what about those Bentley girls? Didn't they ______.
4. Did you ever see a smarter line of soldiers. What a ______!
5. Although it poured with rain, there was still a big ______ for the soccer match.
6. The thieves really ______ his house.
7. He shouldn't have raised the topic at that stage of the meeting. He talked entirely ______.
8. The company should be making a profit within three months. It's ______.

The possibilities: *out of turn, on the turn, turn it on, turn (one) on, turn out, turn over, turn off*

Talk Talk Talk

(Grand Hotel, lobby)

(Grand Hotel, Lobby)

P. Good morning, Archie. You're bright and early. Care for some breakfast before we set off?

P. Guten Morgen, Archie. Sie sind frisch und munter. Möchten Sie etwas frühstücken bevor wir aufbrechen?

A-S. I'll certainly settle for a cup of coffee. Lead the way.

A-S. Ich würde gerne eine Tasse Kaffee trinken. Gehen Sie bitte vor.

P. Oh, Archie, I'd like you to meet my Ergo **colleague**, Don Schering. I invited him along for breakfast.

P. Oh, Archie, ich würde Sie gerne meinem Ergo-**Kollegen** Don Schering vorstellen. Ich habe ihn mit

John, this is Archie Atherton-Smythe. We met on the plane to New York. Archie, let me introduce Ergo's New York **office manager**, Don Schering.

zum Frühstück eingeladen. John, das ist Archie Atherton-Smythe. Wir haben uns im Flugzeug nach New York kennen gelernt. Archie, darf ich Ihnen den Office Manager unserer New Yorker Niederlassung, Don Schering, vorstellen.

A-S. Delighted to meet you, Mr Schering.

A-S. Freut mich, Sie kennen zu lernen, Mr Schering.

D. Oh, call me Don. Everybody else does.

D. Oh, nennen Sie mich Don. Das tut jeder.

A-S. Schering. Are you a compatriot of Peter's?

A-S. Schering. Sind Sie ein Landsmann von Peter?

D. No, I'm American through and through, though I gather my ancestors came over from Peter's home city, Hamburg.

D. Nein, ich bin durch und durch Amerikaner, obwohl ich erfahren habe, dass meine Vorfahren aus Peters Heimatstadt Hamburg kamen.

A-S. How very interesting. My own ancestry is **rooted in** the English soil, though I did spend some time in Hollywood.

A-S. Höchst interessant. Meine eigenen Ahnen sind **mit** der englischen Erde **verwurzelt**, obwohl ich einige Zeit in Hollywood verbracht habe.

D. Hollywood! Were you in the movie business?

D. Hollywood! Waren Sie im Filmgeschäft?

A-S. You could say that. Did you ever see »Moon over the Ganges«?

A-S. Das könnte man so sagen. Haben Sie jemals »Moon over the Ganges« gesehen?

D. Can't say I did. What was it about?

D. Das kann ich nicht behaupten. Worum ging es?

A-S. Well, there was this butler ...

A-S. Nun, da war dieser Butler ...

Train Yourself

Archie tells Peter: »Lead on« – asking him to show the way to the breakfast room. The verb and noun »lead« are used in many common expressions. **In the following sentences, replace the words in italics by using correct forms employing »lead«:**

1. She has been given the *principal role* in the new play.

....

2. The police reported they had an important *clue* in the murder investigation.

....

3. Right, it's time to *start the game*.

....

4. He *enticed her on a wrong course of action.*

....

5. The speaker spent a lot of time *introducing* the main topic of his address.

....

6. They rapidly *took the initiative* in that important contest.

....

Talk Talk Talk

(Grand Hotel, breakfast room)	(Grand Hotel, Frühstückszimmer)
A-S. So come along, Peter. Time to make for the trade fair.	A-S. Auf geht's, Peter. Es wird Zeit, zur Messe aufzubrechen.
P. Righto, Archie! Waiter, can I have the bill, please.	P. In Ordnung, Archie! Herr Ober, kann ich bitte die Rechnung haben.

Waiter: Will you be **signing for** it, sir?

Ober: Wollen Sie sie **abzeichnen**, mein Herr?

P. Yes, please **charge** it to my room. OK, Archie, let's go ...

P. Ja, bitte **setzen** Sie es **auf** meine **Zimmerrechnung**. Alles klar Archie, gehen wir ...

(Trade fair centre)

(Messezentrum)

A-S. We have another half hour before they open the doors. Let's see if Rory and Cliff have turned up yet. Yes, there they are, the dear boys. We're ready to **open** shop.

A-S. Wir haben noch eine halbe Stunde Zeit, bevor die Türen geöffnet werden. Lassen Sie uns mal nachsehen, ob Rory und Cliff schon aufgetaucht sind. Ja, da sind sie ja, die Guten. Jetzt können wir den Laden **öffnen**.

P. What can I do?

P. Was kann ich tun?

A-S. Oh, just look around the fair at your leisure and look by occasionally to see if we need **reinforcements**. But be here at eleven because we have a small **reception** for some important **clients**.

A-S. Oh, wenn es Ihnen passt, dann sehen Sie sich einfach auf der Messe um und schauen Sie ab und zu vorbei, um zu sehen, ob wir **Verstärkung** brauchen. Aber seien Sie um elf Uhr da, weil wir einen kleinen **Empfang** für ein paar wichtige **Kunden** haben.

P. Righto, see you later ...

P. In Ordnung, bis später ...

P. Sorry I'm late Archie. I got bogged down at a German **manufacturer's stand**.

P. Entschuldigen Sie die Verspätung, Archie. Ich bin beim **Messestand** eines deutschen **Herstellers** stecken geblieben.

A-S. Did you pick up any hints? What are they **showing**?

A-S. Haben Sie ein paar Hinweise aufgeschnappt? Was **stellen** sie **aus**?

P. I brought all this **information material** for you, Archie. They're not in direct **competition** with you and would actually like to meet you.

P. Ich habe Ihnen dieses ganze **Informationsmaterial** mitgebracht, Archie. Sie sind keine direkte **Konkurrenz** für Sie und würden Sie wirklich gerne kennen lernen.

A-S. Take me round there this afternoon, Peter. You can help me entertain this crowd right now ...

A-S. Stellen Sie mich heute Nachmittag vor, Peter. Jetzt können Sie mir helfen, diese Bande hier zu unterhalten ...

Client: Mr Atherton-Smythe tells me you are from Germany. I must say I've long admired German banking practice, and it can be no coincidence that the new European Central Bank has its headquarters in Frankfurt.

Kunde: Mr Atherton-Smythe sagte mir, dass Sie aus Deutschland sind. Ich muss sagen, dass ich die deutschen Bankpraktiken seit langem bewundere und es kein Zufall sein kann, dass die neue Europäische Zentralbank ihren Hauptsitz in Frankfurt hat.

P. Oh, London **put up some stiff competition** for that honour, don't forget.

P. Oh, bei dieser Ehre hat sich London **als harte Konkurrenz erwiesen**, vergessen Sie das nicht.

Second client: Mr Atherton-Smythe says you are at present working in London, in the **high-tech branch**.

Zweiter Kunde: Mr Atherton-Smythe sagte, Sie würden momentan in London arbeiten, in der **Hightechbranche**.

P. Yes, that's right. I'm with Ergo Limited. We like to think we'**re leaders in our field**.

P. Ja, das ist richtig. Ich bin bei Ergo Limited. Wir **sind** – unserer Meinung nach – **führend auf diesem Gebiet**.

Second Client: You must tell me more about your **company** – that is, if you have the time.

Zweiter Kunde: Sie müssen mir mehr über Ihr **Unternehmen** erzählen – das heißt, wenn Sie Zeit haben.

P. Certainly, do join me for a cup of coffee, and I'll do my best. Archie, is it all right if I take a corner of your stand for ten minutes or so?

P. Natürlich, trinken Sie mit mir eine Tasse Kaffee und ich werde mein Bestes geben. Archie, ist es in Ordnung, wenn ich für ungefähr zehn Minuten eine Ecke Ihres Messestandes beanspruche?

A-S. Certainly. Make yourself at home ...

A-S. Natürlich. Fühlen Sie sich wie zu Hause ...

False Friends

The client at the Royal Star Banking **stand** tells Peter: »I must say I've long admired German banking practice«. He is not saying he is under pressure to make the compliment, but is expressing enthusiasm. A young woman who hears the words: »I must say you look especially beautiful in that dress« is receiving a compliment. So is the dinner-party hostess who is told by a guest: »I must say that meal was marvellous.« But be careful – if you are told »You must admit you made a big mistake« you're getting no compliment.

Train Yourself

Put the following sentences using the verb »must« into the tense indicated:

1. They must complete the accounts before going on holiday (*simple past*).

....

2. Must I really complete this work by the end of the week (*future*)?

....

3. We thought we just must see the show, so we went last Tuesday (*simple past*).

....

4. If they want to reach Jamestown by nightfall they must take the lower road (*future*).

5. If they really think they must move out then that's all right by me (*simple past*).

6. The company must put its books in order if it wants to avoid bankruptcy (*future*).

Talk Talk Talk

Client: Thank you, Mr – er. **I do beg your pardon**, I don't think I know your name.

Kunde: Ich danke Ihnen, Mr – ähm. **Verzeihen Sie**, ich glaube, ich kenne Ihren Namen nicht.

P. Brückner. Peter Brückner.

P. Brückner. Peter Brückner.

Client: Jack Dawson. **It's been a pleasure talking to you**, Mr Brückner. Here's my **card**.

Kunde: Jack Dawson. **Es war mir ein Vergnügen, mich mit Ihnen zu unterhalten**, Mr Brückner. Hier ist meine **Karte**.

P. And do take mine. **I'll be pleased to see you** if ever you get over to London. If you ever have to go to Germany I can put you in touch with some useful **contacts** there, too.

P. Und hier ist meine. **Es würde mich freuen, Sie wiederzusehen**, wenn Sie jemals nach London kommen. Sollten Sie jemals nach Deutschland müssen, kann ich Sie auch dort mit einigen nützlichen **Kontakten** zusammenbringen.

A-S. Ah, here you are, Peter. I have a **spare** half-hour. Can you take me to meet your German contact?

A-S. Ah, hier sind Sie, Peter. Ich habe eine halbe Stunde **frei**. Können Sie mich zu Ihrem deutschen Kontakt bringen?

P. Certainly, Archie. His company's stand is F-15. It's this way ...

P. Natürlich Archie. Die Standnummer seiner Firma ist F-15. Hier entlang ...

P. Archie, I'd like you to meet Gerhard Huber, **managing director** of Schmidt Sicherheitssysteme. Herr Huber, this is Mr Archie Atherton-Smythe.

P. Archie, ich möchte Ihnen Gerhard Huber vorstellen, den **Geschäftsführer** von Schmidt Sicherheitssysteme. Herr Huber, das ist Mr Archie Atherton-Smythe.

H. I'm very pleased to meet you, Mr Atherton-Smythe. Herr Brückner says you **have a** very successful **company** which is concerned with **banking security**.

H. Sehr erfreut, Sie kennen zu lernen, Mr Atherton-Smythe. Herr Brückner sagt, Sie **haben eine** sehr erfolgreiche **Firma**, die sich um **Bankensicherheit** kümmert.

A-S. Well, that's very kind of him. We have some **stiff competition**, but we do **believe** strongly **in our product**.

A-S. Nun, das ist nett von ihm. Wir haben einige **harte Konkurrenten**, aber wir **glauben** fest **an unser Produkt**.

H. I'd be honoured if you looked around our stand. But do let me invite you to a pre-lunch snack.

H. Es wäre mir eine Ehre, wenn Sie bei unserem Messestand vorbeischauten. Aber darf ich Sie vor dem Mittagessen noch zu einem Snack einladen.

Train Yourself

Peter replies »Certainly« when Archie asks if he can take him to the German stand at the trade fair. He means: »Certainly I can« or »Certainly I will«, using the adverbial form of »certain«. If Peter asks Archie if he knows a »certain« person at the fair he uses the word in his adjectival form. **Find the correct form in the following sentences:**

1. Are you ____________ this is the way? ____________ I'm very sure indeed.

2. He ______ knows how to paint. His pictures are ______ ______ to fetch good prices at auction.
3. Is it ______ he is to be sacked? Are you quite sure?
4. She's a lady of a ______ age, if you know what I mean. She's ______ to take offence if you ask her just how old she is.
5. I can ______ help you in this matter, but you have to be ______ you want to proceed.
6. It's ______ a difficult case to take on, but if you're ______ I am the right man then I'll ______ try.

Talk Talk Talk

P. Well, Mr Huber. That was most interesting. You certainly have a very fine **product** there.

P. Nun, Herr Huber. Das war höchst interessant. Sie haben hier mit Sicherheit ein sehr gutes **Produkt**.

A-S. Yes, indeed! And your stand is extremely well designed. It has given me some ideas for our next **trade fair appearance**. And your **display** of your **products** is most tastefully done. I must congratulate you.

A-S. Ja, tatsächlich! Und Ihr Stand wurde ausgesprochen gut konstruiert. Das hat mich auf ein paar Ideen für unseren nächsten **Messeauftritt** gebracht. Und Ihre **Produktpräsentation** ist sehr geschmackvoll. Ich muss Ihnen gratulieren.

H. I would be happy to meet you perhaps in England and **discuss a possible co-operation**.

H. Es würde mich freuen, Sie eventuell in England zu treffen und **eine mögliche Zusammenarbeit zu besprechen.**

A-S. Any time, Mr Huber. Any time. I shall be glad to welcome you at Royal Star Banking.

A-S. Jederzeit, Herr Huber. Jederzeit. Ich würde mich freuen, Sie bei Royal Star Banking empfangen zu dürfen.

H. A royal welcome! I would certainly like that. Well, goodbye!

H. Ein königlicher Empfang! Das würde mich auf jeden Fall freuen.

I hope to see you again before long.

Nun, auf Wiedersehen! Ich hoffe, Sie bald wieder zu sehen.

A-S. Come along, Peter. We still have a busy day ahead of us, and a dinner to attend this evening ...

A-S. Kommen Sie, Peter. Wir haben noch einen anstrengenden Tag vor uns und ein Abendessen, an dem wir heute Abend teilnehmen müssen ...

False Friends

Be careful not to confuse the words **»attend«** and **»intend«**. Archie tells Peter they must attend a dinner that evening, meaning they have to be present. He intends to be there, meaning he plans or proposes to go.

Train Yourself

The verb »attend« actually has several meanings. **Replace the words in italics in the following sentences with correct forms of the verb »attend«:**

1. *Were you present at* the awards ceremony last night?

2. I was there, but I was so tired I didn't *pay much attention* to what was said.

3. John, could you *look after* that client for me?

4. My brother-in-law is a forester and *looks after* the state national park.

5. Which university is your son *going to* now?

6. My medical specialist also *looks after* ear, nose and throat patients.

Talk Talk Talk

A-S. Well, thank you most sincerely for your **assistance**, Peter, my dear chap. It was most useful.

A-S. Nun, ich danke Ihnen aufrichtig für Ihre **Unterstützung**, Peter, mein lieber Junge. Das hat mir sehr geholfen.

P. **Don't mention it**, Archie. I thoroughly enjoyed the experience.

P. **Nicht der Rede wert**, Archie. Ich habe diese Erfahrung genossen.

A-S. Then I'll meet you in the lobby of the Lexington Hotel at seven this evening?

A-S. Dann treffe ich Sie heute Abend um sieben Uhr in der Lobby des Lexington Hotels?

P. Yes, I'll be there. I'm very much looking forward to it ...

P. Ja, ich werde dort sein. Ich freue mich schon sehr darauf ...

(Lexington Hotel, lobby)

(Lexington Hotel, Lobby)

A-S. Hello there, Peter! Right on time! No wonder the Germans know how to **keep to** a railway timetable.

A-S. Hallo Peter! Gerade zur rechten Zeit! Kein Wunder, dass die Deutschen wissen, wie man einen Zugfahrplan **einhält**.

P. Not always, Archie, I do assure you.

P. Nicht immer, Archie, das kann ich Ihnen versichern.

A-S. Ah, there's Rosemary Day. I met her at the trade fair yesterday. She does something important in a big **export-import enterprise** in Boston. You must meet her. Rosemary! How nice to see you again!

A-S. Ah, dort ist Rosemary Day. Ich habe sie gestern auf der Messe kennen gelernt. Sie macht irgendetwas Wichtiges in einem großen **Export-Import-Unternehmen** in Boston. Sie müssen sie kennen lernen. Rosemary! Wie schön, Sie wieder zu sehen!

R. Archie! I didn't know you intend-

R. Archie! Ich wusste nicht, dass

ed to be at the dinner.

Sie vorhatten, beim Abendessen dabei zu sein.

A-S. I attend any function which promises a five-course meal and a cocktail to start with. Some of my colleagues call me a **professional freeloader**. What table have you been allotted? Six? Same as us – do join us.

A-S. Ich wohne jeder Feierlichkeit bei, die ein Fünf-Gänge-Menü und einen Cocktail als Aperitif verspricht. Einige meiner Kollegen nennen mich einen **professionellen Schnorrer**. Welcher Tisch ist Ihnen zugewiesen worden? Sechs? Derselbe wie uns – leisten Sie uns doch Gesellschaft.

Train Yourself

Archie tells Peter he doesn't find it surprising the Germans keep to a railway timetable – referring to the English belief that German trains always run on time! »Keep to« means to abide by, to adhere to – »He kept to his promise«. There are several other useful expressions employing the verb »keep« – **find the correct ones with which to replace the words in italics in the following sentences:**

1. He's totally unsuitable for that job. He *makes one mistake after the other.*

....

2. If you want to achieve something in life you just have to *persevere.*

....

3. We've been broken into twice in the past month, so when we go away this weekend please *watch* the house for us.

....

4. The boss is very angry this morning, so it's advisable to *stay out of sight.*

....

5. You don't have to be so angry. Can't you *control your temper?*

6. We *gathered together* once a week at soirées where we liked to chat and perhaps play a little bridge.

7. She's a very shy young woman and prefers to *lead a solitary life.*

8. This is a very secret recipe. Please *don't divulge it.*

Talk Talk Talk

A-S. So, dear friends ... I hope I may call you that. What about starters?	A-S. So, liebe Freunde ... ich hoffe, ich darf Sie so nennen. Wie wäre es mit einer Vorspeise?
R. Tell me, Archie, how do you think the trade fair is going?	R. Sagen Sie mir, Archie, wie glauben Sie läuft die Messe?
A-S. The fair – or our **performance** there?	A-S. Die Messe – oder unser **Auftritt** dort?
R. Well, both really.	R. Nun, beides natürlich.
A-S. Do you know, I think the best person to answer your question is Peter. He's the independent observer.	A-S. Wissen Sie was, ich glaube, die geeignetste Person, um Ihre Frage zu beantworten, ist Peter. Er ist ein unabhängiger Beobachter.
P. I found the trade fair itself very interesting, and I shall be surprised if Archie's presence did not **produce new business**.	P. Ich fand die Messe selbst sehr interessant, und es würde mich wundern, wenn Archies Anwesenheit nicht **zu neuen Geschäften geführt hat**.

A-S. Peter, I wish I could share your confidence. I rather feel the Americans have **stolen a march** on us. Their stands are far more professional.

A-S. Peter, ich wünschte, ich könnte Ihre Zuversicht teilen. Ich habe eher das Gefühl, die Amerikaner haben **uns die Schau gestohlen**. Ihre Messestände sind weitaus professioneller.

P. Yes, but that's precisely what visitors like about your stand, Archie. It's so traditional. You **can't fail** in America, anyway, with »Royal« as part of your **logo**.

P. Ja, aber genau das ist es, was Besucher an Ihrem Stand mögen, Archie. Er ist so traditionell. Außerdem **können Sie** in Amerika mit »Royal« – »Königlich« – als Teil Ihres Logos **nicht versagen**.

A-S. Logo, logo? There's nothing royal about a logo. But I get your point, dear boy. I get your point. Now, what's the main course?

A-S. Logo, Logo? An einem Logo ist nichts königlich. Aber ich verstehe, was Sie meinen, mein Lieber. Nun, was gibt es als Hauptgericht?

R. Archie, you've forgotten the soup. And do you know what it is? Royal Windsor ...

R. Archie, Sie haben die Suppe vergessen. Und wissen Sie, welche es ist? Royal Windsor ...

A-S. Bound to be good, Rosemary. It just has to be delicious ...

A-S. Die muss ja gut sein, Rosemary. Sie muss einfach köstlich sein ...

Train Yourself

Multiple choice

Let's do some revision now of our knowledge of prepositions. **Select the correct prepositions in the following sentences:**

1. During her time at university she trained __________ the art of tapestry (*for, in, at, with*).
2. He followed __________ his job application with a personal phone call to the managing director (*on, with, up, out*).

3. They can't make ______ their minds (*up, for, on, with*) ______ (*up, for, on, with*) where to take their holidays this year.
4. The company decided ______ a stringent policy of across-the-board economies (*for, at, on, with*).
5. When you finally arrive ______ a solution please give us a call (*on, for, at, with*).
6. When you have chosen ______ the products you like best we shall be glad to take your order (*on, for, –, at*).

Talk Talk Talk

R. (whispers to Archie) The man sitting opposite you is the Argentinian representative of a big South American **finance house**. He's quite famous, but very shy. I'd like to **involve him in our conversation**, but frankly I believe he's terrified of women.

R. (flüstert zu Archie) Der Mann, der Ihnen gegenübersitzt, ist der argentinische Vertreter eines großen südamerikanischen **Finanzhauses**. Er ist ziemlich berühmt, aber sehr schüchtern. Ich würde ihn gerne **in unser Gespräch einbeziehen**, aber ehrlich gesagt glaube ich, er hat Angst vor Frauen.

A-S. Leave it to me, dear lady. Leave it to me ... Nice drop of wine, this. Do you know, I believe it's South American, but for the life of me I can't read the **label**. These glasses of mine are no good at all. I gather you are from Argentina, sir. Perhaps you could help me out.

A-S. Überlassen Sie das mir, meine Liebe. Überlassen Sie das mir ... Das ist ein guter Tropfen Wein. Wissen Sie, ich glaube er kommt aus Südamerika, aber ich kann das **Etikett** nicht lesen, und wenn es um mein Leben ginge. Meine Brille ist überhaupt nicht gut. Mein Herr, ich höre, Sie kommen aus Argentinien. Vielleicht können Sie mir weiterhelfen.

Señor Rodriguez de Torres: Certainly, señor. If you would be so kind as to pass me the bottle. You must know your wine, señor. This

Señor Rodriguez de Torres: Natürlich, Señor. Wenn Sie so freundlich wären und mir die Flasche reichen. Sie müssen Ihren

is from Chile. Not Argentinian, alas, although we produce some fine wines.

Wein schon kennen, Señor. Dieser hier ist aus Chile. Es ist kein argentinischer, leider, obwohl wir sehr guten Wein herstellen.

A-S. I know, indeed. I frequently serve up Argentinian wine at my little soirées in London.

A-S. Das weiß ich in der Tat. Ich serviere oft argentinischen Wein bei meinen kleinen Soireen in London.

RT. Ah, you are from London?

RT. Ah, Sie kommen aus London?

A-S. Yes, like my friend, Mr Brückner, although he is German.

A-S. Ja, wie mein Freund Herr Brückner, obwohl er Deutscher ist.

RT. And the lady, **I take it**, is American?

RT. Und die Dame ist, **nehme ich an**, Amerikanerin?

R. Yes, born and bred right here in New York.

R. Ja, geboren und aufgewachsen direkt hier in New York.

RT. Then we really are a multinational table. May I propose a toast among us to cordial **international relations**.

RT. Dann sind wir wirklich ein multinationaler Tisch. Darf ich einen Trinkspruch aussprechen auf herzliche **internationale Beziehungen** zwischen uns.

A-S. You may certainly do that, dear sir. Here's to a better international climate – particularly between your country and mine.

A-S. Mein lieber Herr, das dürfen Sie sicherlich tun. Auf ein besseres internationales Klima – besonders zwischen Ihrem Land und meinem.

R. (between clenched teeth) Archie, the Falklands war has been over for a very long time now ...

R. (mit zusammengebissenen Zähnen) Archie, der Falklandkrieg ist jetzt schon sehr lange vorbei ...

Background Information

A point of etiquette

In **striking up a conversation** with a stranger seek out **a topic of common interest**. It's no longer sufficient, even in Britain, to make a lame comment on the weather and expect the exchange to continue. Archie finds an **ideal opening** – a wine bottle – but then takes an undiplomatic line which could lead him into deep water!

Train Yourself

You, a German businessperson, are alone at a banquet being given in honour of a visiting British politician. You are at a table full of British business people. They all know each other, and although they smile politely at you they otherwise exhibit typical English reserve. You take stock of what you have in order to join in the conversation:

1. Business cards
2. An identity tag on your lapel
3. An interest in the company represented by one of the British business people at the table
4. A previous chance meeting with the British politician guest of honour
5. You sometimes play golf with the British Consul General
6. Your wife/husband works for a British concern

How would you »play these cards« in order to enter the conversation? **Develop a strategy that would give you entry to the circle of business people ...**

....

....

....

....

Talk Talk Talk

A-S. When do you leave for London, Peter?

A-S. Peter, wann reisen Sie nach London ab?

P. The day after tomorrow, Archie.

P. Übermorgen, Archie.

A-S. I'm here until the following week, you know. So we must have a little farewell party. It'll be an **impromptu** one, but I'll call around and see if people are free tomorrow evening. Unless you have something else in mind?

A-S. Ich bin bis nächste Woche hier, wissen Sie. Also müssen wir eine kleine Abschiedsparty machen. Es wird eine **improvisierte** sein, aber ich werde herumtelefonieren und schauen, ob die Leute morgen Abend Zeit haben. Wenn Sie nichts anderes im Sinn haben?

P. No, Archie. I'd like that.

P. Nein Archie, das würde mir Spaß machen.

A-S. I have tomorrow afternoon off, so let's make one last excursion together. Do you know Staten Island?

A-S. Morgen Nachmittag habe ich frei, lassen Sie uns also einen letzten Ausflug zusammen machen. Kennen Sie Staten Island?

P. I know it's there, but I haven't been.

P. Ich weiß, dass es das gibt, aber ich bin noch nicht dort gewesen.

A-S. It's not the island that's so interesting, but the means of getting there and back – by ferry. If you want to get to know a city on the water then take to a boat. Look at Hong Kong, Bangkok – the great waterside cities of the east. I'll **pick** you **up** at the hotel at two o'clock.

A-S. Die Insel ist nicht so interessant, aber die Art und Weise wie man hin- und zurückkommt – mit der Fähre. Wenn Sie eine Stadt am Wasser kennen lernen wollen, dann greifen Sie zu einem Boot. Sehen Sie sich Hongkong, Bangkok an – die großen Städte des Ostens am Wasser. Ich **hole** Sie um zwei Uhr vom Hotel **ab**.

Train Yourself

There are various forms of the verb »take«. Archie introduces us here to one by advising Peter to »take to« a boat in order to get to know New York better. **In the following sentences, replace the words in italics with forms of the verb »take«:**

1. Admiral Jameson has *assumed command* of the fleet.

2. The best way to get to their offices is to *travel on* the District Line as far as Victoria, then walk.

3. My son is growing so fast that he already *needs* a size nine shoe.

4. He *is certainly very leisurely* in completing that job of work.

5. You two can complete the task more easily by *doing it alternately.*

6. I really must *disagree with* your reasoning on that topic.

7. They originally came to the town for six months but they've now *put down roots.*

8. Since Johnson took over at the company Smith has had to *assume a secondary role* in running things.

Vocabulary

assistance	Unterstützung
a tall order	ein bisschen viel verlangt
at your leisure	wenn es Ihnen passt
banking security	Bankensicherheit
to bargain	verhandeln
to be leaders in a field	führend auf einem Gebiet sein
to believe in a product	an ein Produkt glauben
can't fail	nicht versagen können
card	Visitenkarte
to charge	auf die Rechnung setzen
client	Kunde
colleague	Kollege
company	Unternehmen
competition	Konkurrenz
contact	Kontakt
to discuss a possible co-operation	über eine mögliche Zusammenarbeit sprechen
display of products	Produktpräsentation
to drive a hard bargain	harte Verhandlungen führen
export-import enterprise	Export-Import-Unternehmen
to have a company	für eine Firma arbeiten
to have a reception for somebody	für jemanden einen Empfang geben
How do you do?	Guten Tag.
I take it	ich nehme an (Vermutung)
I'm delighted to meet you.	Erfreut, Sie kennen zu lernen.
impromptu	improvisiert
I'd like you to meet ...	Ich möchte, dass Sie ... kennen lernen.
in return	im Gegenzug
to be in the market for	auf dem Markt sein mit
information material	Informationsmaterial
international relations	internationale Beziehungen
to keep to	etwas einhalten
let me introduce you to ...	lassen Sie mich Ihnen ... vorstellen

logo	Logo
to look around a stand	bei einem Messestand vorbeischauen
to manage	hinbekommen, schaffen
managing director	Geschäftsführer
office manager	Office Manager
manufacturer	Hersteller
to open	eröffnen, aufmachen
overdraft	Überziehungssumme
to pick somebody up	jemanden abholen
to produce new business	zu neuen Geschäften führen
product	Produkt
professional freeloader	professioneller Schnorrer
reinforcement	Verstärkung
to represent one's company	seine Firma vertreten
rooted in	verwurzelt mit
to show	ausstellen
to sign for	abzeichnen, unterschreiben
to spare	ersparen
stand	Messestand
to steal a march on	dabei die Schau stehlen
stiff competition	harte Konkurrenz
to take a look at one's company's operation	einen Blick auf die Tätigkeiten seiner Firma werfen
trade fair	Messe/Fachmesse
trade fair appearance/performance	Messeauftritt
trade fair stand	Messestand

The enterprise
Das Unternehmen

Here we go

Jetzt ist Archie an der Reihe, Peter New York zu zeigen – und sie haben die Gelegenheit, ein paar wichtige Geschäftsinformationen auszutauschen. Am nächsten Tag muss Peter nach London zurückkehren, nach einer letzten Verabschiedung am Flughafen ...

Talk Talk Talk

(Grand Hotel, lobby)	(Grand Hotel, Lobby)
P. Hello Archie, **good to see you again**.	P. Hallo Archie, **schön Sie wieder zu sehen**.
A-S. Hello Peter, all ready for the voyage?	A-S. Hallo Peter, alles fertig für die Reise?
P. Voyage, Archie?	P. Reise, Archie?
A-S. Well, it's a good hour there, and another hour back again.	A-S. Nun ja, es ist eine gute Stunde hin, und eine Stunde zurück.
P. Then let's embark ...	P. Dann lassen Sie uns an Bord gehen ...
P. We're passing very close to the Statue of Liberty. This is a view I missed on the plane.	P. Wir fahren ganz dicht an der Freiheitsstatue vorbei. Das ist ein Anblick, den ich im Flugzeug verpasst habe.
A-S. And this view is **for free**. Quite	A-S. Und dieser Anblick ist **um-**

a sight, isn't it? ... Here we are then. We've just time for a coffee at a diner I know up the road, before heading back.

sonst. Eine ganz tolle Aussicht, nicht wahr? ... Da sind wir also. Bevor wir umkehren, haben wir gerade Zeit für einen Kaffee in einem Lokal, das ich in der Nähe kenne.

P. Archie, for a visitor you know New York very well.

P. Archie, für einen Besucher kennen Sie New York sehr gut.

A-S. I've been here several times before, remember.

A-S. Ich bin ja schon einige Male hier gewesen.

False Friends

Take care with the word **»quite«**. It can give the word it qualifies the meaning of something outstanding – or quite the reverse. Its principal meaning is **»completely«** or **»wholly«** – »I shall be quite finished with that job of work within an hour«, »Are you quite sure?«. Archie tells Peter the view of the Statue of Liberty from the Staten Island ferry is »quite a sight« – meaning it's a very fine sight. But in certain circumstances, and particularly when stressed, »quite« can have anything but positive connotations: »How did you like the meal?« »Well, I suppose it was quite nice.« (It probably was a disaster!) »What's John's new girlfriend like?« »She's quite pretty.« (She's probably very unattractive).

Train Yourself

Let's take a good look now at some uses of the adjective »good«. **In the following sentences, replace the words in italics with expressions employing »good«:**

1. Although the car has 100,000 kilometers on the clock, I think *it can last for* another 100,000 without problem.

....

2. Why did you recommend that young fellow? He's *totally useless.*

....

3. At this rate, it will take *at least another hour* to get home.

....

4. She's a very talented writer, very *adroit* with the pen.

....

5. He's extremely *knowledgeable* on mechanical things, like steam engines and old factory equipment.

....

6. *Several* of us were kept waiting for the doctor to arrive.

....

7. The two partners have *finally split up*. They've said goodbye to each other once and for all.

....

8. Well, I suppose it's *for the best.*

....

Talk Talk Talk

(Diner)

A-S. I always have to remind myself in any of my dealings here in the States that the Americans are expected to work longer hours than is the rule in Europe. Even in the business world – particularly in business, I would say. And two weeks **annual holiday** is still the rule here. How is it in Germany?

(Speiselokal)

A-S. Bei meinen Geschäftsaktivitäten hier in den Staaten, muss ich mir immer wieder bewusst machen, dass von den Amerikanern grundsätzlich eine längere Stundenwoche erwartet wird, als sie in Europa üblich ist, sogar, oder vor allem, in der Businesswelt, würde ich sagen. Ein zweiwöchiger **Jahresurlaub** ist hier immer noch die Regel. Wie sieht es in Deutschland aus?

P. Germans can certainly expect more annual holiday. Four weeks is the norm, and six weeks is also not unusual. And in Britain?

P. Die Deutschen können sicherlich mehr erwarten. Vier Wochen Jahresurlaub sind normal, und sechs Wochen sind auch nicht unüblich. Und wie ist es in Großbritannien?

A-S. About the same. But shorter **working hours** and longer holiday entitlements were achieved through considerable **union** pressure, and that's always impressed me about Germany. I think your unions don't need to flex their muscle much.

A-S. Sehr ähnlich. Aber kürzere **Arbeitszeiten** und längere Ferien wurden immer erst durch erheblichen Druck seitens der **Gewerkschaften** erreicht, und das hat mich immer so sehr an Deutschland fasziniert. Ich glaube, die Gewerkschaften müssen hier nicht so sehr dafür kämpfen.

P. Things are changing on that front, too, Archie. **Strikes** are by no means an uncommon occurrence in Germany now.

P. Dies ändert sich allerdings auch an dieser Front, Archie. **Streiks** sind überhaupt keine Seltenheit mehr in Deutschland.

A-S. Oh, I know. I recall reading about some spectacular **industrial actions** in your country, too. Time to take the ferry back. The sun's going down.

A-S. Oh ja, ich weiß. Ich erinnere mich, Berichte über spektakuläre **Arbeitskämpfe** auch in Ihrem Land gelesen zu haben. Zeit, die Fähre zurück zu nehmen. Die Sonne geht schon unter.

P. **Let me pay for this**, Archie.

P. **Lassen Sie mich das bezahlen**, Archie.

A-S. If you insist. Many thanks. It's only a ten minute walk down to the ferry station ...

A-S. Wenn Sie darauf bestehen. Vielen Dank. Es ist nur ein Spaziergang von zehn Minuten zur Anlegestelle hinunter ...

Train Yourself

Archie reminds himself of certain facts here. He remembers or recalls them. Remind, remember, recall – three similar words requiring careful attention. **Fill the gaps in the following sentences with the correct ones:**

1. Let me ________ for you the events of that evening.
2. May I ________ you of your duty to queen and country?
3. Don't you ________ me? We were in the same graduation class.
4. His style of painting ________ the pre-Raphaelites.
5. He ________ me very much of his father.
6. ________ me to your parents.
7. ________, ________, the Fifth of November. Gunpowder, treason and plot. This old rhyme ________ Guy Fawkes's attempt to blow up Parliament.
8. The old man ________ her in his will and left her a sizeable inheritance.

Talk Talk Talk

A-S. Here we are, there's a boat in – let's take that.

A-S. Da sind wir, dort liegt ein Boot – lassen Sie uns das nehmen.

P. I see why you like to take an evening ferry back to Manhattan. Just look at those lights coming on. It's quite magical ...

P. Ich verstehe, warum Sie gerne eine Abendfähre zurück nach Manhattan nehmen. Sehen Sie sich nur die Lichter an, die jetzt überall angehen. Das ist ganz wundervoll ...

A-S. Well, that didn't take long, did it? Not even time enough to get seasick. **I'd like to show you** Lower Manhattan, and we could have supper in Chinatown. I know

A-S. Nun, das hat nicht lang gedauert, nicht wahr? Nicht einmal lang genug, um seekrank zu werden. **Ich würde Ihnen gerne** Lower Manhattan **zeigen**, wir könnten in

an excellent and very authentic restaurant there.

Chinatown zu Abend essen. Ich kenne dort ein ausgezeichnetes und authentisches Restaurant.

P. Archie, I'm in your hands.

P. Archie, ich bin in Ihrer Hand.

A-S. We'll ride the subway one stop and then I'll take you down Wall Street. From there we can get a cab to Chinatown.

A-S. Wir fahren eine Station mit der U-Bahn und dann zeige ich Ihnen die Wall Street. Von dort können wir ein Taxi nach Chinatown nehmen.

P. **Fine by me**, Archie.

P. **Einverstanden**, Archie.

A-S. There's just one problem ...

A-S. Da gibt es nur ein Problem ...

P. And that is?

P. Und das ist?

A-S. I've forgotten where the next subway stop is. I'll ask this newspaper vendor. Excuse me, could you direct me to the nearest subway station ...

A-S. Ich habe vergessen, wo die nächste U-Bahn-Station ist. Ich frage den Zeitungsverkäufer hier. Entschuldigen Sie, könnten Sie mir sagen, wo die nächste U-Bahn-Station ist ...

P. What did he say?

P. Was hat er gesagt?

A-S. I had to repeat it three times. The chap said he couldn't understand a word I said. Something to do with my accent. But the subway is this way ...

A-S. Ich musste es dreimal wiederholen. Der Typ sagte, er könnte mich nicht verstehen. Hätte etwas mit meinem Akzent zu tun. Aber zur U-Bahn geht es hier entlang ...

Train Yourself

Finding your way around

You are staying at a hotel on 44th Street, Manhattan. A business colleague is staying at a hotel on 56th Street. You arrange to meet in a bar at the corner of 50th Street and Lexington Avenue, which cuts through both streets. You ask the hotel desk clerk for directions to the bar and he says: »Turn right outside the hotel, carry straight on until you reach Lexington Avenue, again take a right turn and carry straight on until you reach 50th Street, you'll see the bar on the corner.« Your business colleague, coming from the other direction, also asks the desk clerk at his hotel for directions. **What does the desk clerk tell him?**

....

....

....

....

....

Talk Talk Talk

A-S. Here we are. The restaurant is there on the right.	A-S. Da sind wir. Das Restaurant ist dort rechts.
P. What a fascinating district. We could be in Hong Kong.	P. Was für ein faszinierendes Viertel. Wir könnten in Hongkong sein.
A-S. More authentic than Hong Kong. There are no highrises here, no American fast-food outlets. This is your real China. Now, come along inside – I hope you like Cantonese food.	A-S. Authentischer als Hongkong. Hier gibt es keine Hochhäuser, keine amerikanischen Fastfood-Filialen. Das ist das wahre China. Kommen Sie jetzt mit rein – ich hoffe, Sie mögen kantonesisches Essen.
P. I must confess I haven't had much experience of it ...	P. Ich muss gestehen, dass ich damit noch nicht viel Erfahrung gemacht habe ...

A-S. Then you're **in for** an experience here. **Leave the ordering to me** ... So, tell me a little more about yourself. We've been so busy with business that I still don't really know you. How long have you been in London?

A-S. Dann **steht** Ihnen hier eine neue Erfahrung **bevor**. **Überlassen Sie das Bestellen mir** ... So, erzählen Sie mir ein bisschen mehr über sich. Wir waren so mit Geschäften beschäftigt, dass ich Sie noch nicht wirklich kenne. Seit wann sind Sie in London?

P. Only a few months. When I get back I shall be moving to Glasgow, to **take over Ergo operations** there.

P. Erst ein paar Monate. Wenn ich zurück bin, soll ich nach Glasgow ziehen, um dort **die Geschäfte von Ergo zu übernehmen**.

A-S. Is the family with you in Britain?

A-S. Ist die Familie bei Ihnen in England?

P. I'm unmarried, Archie. Now that I did tell you.

P. Ich bin ledig, Archie. Das habe ich Ihnen aber erzählt.

A-S. Well, you certainly indicated it in the presence of certain young ladies here in New York. What do you do with yourself in London when you're not working?

A-S. Nun ja, das haben Sie in Anwesenheit gewisser junger Damen hier in New York angedeutet. Was treiben Sie so in London, wenn Sie nicht arbeiten?

P. I follow cultural events pretty closely and I spend hours in the museums and art galleries. They really are outstanding in London.

P. Ich halte mich bezüglich kultureller Veranstaltungen ziemlich auf dem Laufenden und verbringe Stunden in Museen und Kunstgalerien. Sie sind wirklich herausragend in London.

A-S. Good to hear. I did art history at university before **going into banking** and then **e-commerce**.

A-S. Schön zu hören. Ich hatte Kunstgeschichte an der Universität studiert, bevor ich mich **dem Bankwesen** und dann dem **E-Commerce gewidmet** habe.

Train Yourself

At the Chinese restaurant, Archie tells Peter to leave the ordering to him. **Replace the words in italics with alternative expressions employing »leave«:**

1. She *bequeathed* several hundred pounds to her niece in her will.

....

2. I wish that boy would *stop teasing my dog.*

....

3. We are looking for some peace and quiet. Would you please *go away.*

....

4. There's only so much one can plan ahead – the rest we'll have *to let* providence *handle.*

....

5. That accident *gave him* a very nasty scar.

....

6. You can do the packing, but *let me handle* the rest of the preparations.

....

7. John's death was a big blow. He *had* a charming wife and three lovely children.

....

8. He's a very bright boy. He *finished* university with a double first.

....

Talk Talk Talk

P. Well, Archie, I must say that was quite a meal. I've never eaten

P. Nun, Archie, ich muss sagen, das war ein tolles Essen. Ich habe better at a Chinese restaurant.

niemals besser gespeist in einem chinesischen Restaurant.

A-S. Oh, I must invite you to lunch in London. I have a favourite place in Soho that puts this **in the shade**.

A-S. Oh, ich muss Sie in London zum Mittagessen einladen. Ich habe ein Lieblingsrestaurant in Soho, das dieses hier **in den Schatten** stellt.

P. I look forward to it, Archie. **I do hope we stay in contact** when we return to Britain.

P. Ich freue mich darauf, Archie. **Ich hoffe sehr, wir bleiben in Kontakt**, wenn wir nach England zurückkehren.

A-S. Without a doubt. And, of course, if you find yourself in Buckinghamshire you are very welcome at my modest country seat. I'd like to show you round my wine cellar. I'm sure it's nothing by German standards, but I am rather proud of my small collection of Bordeaux vintages ...

A-S. Ohne Zweifel. Und wenn Sie in Buckinghamshire sind, sind Sie natürlich herzlich willkommen auf meinem bescheidenen Landsitz. Ich würde Sie gerne in meinem Weinkeller herumführen. Ich bin mir sicher, er ist nichts verglichen mit deutschen Standards, aber ich bin ziemlich stolz auf meine kleine Sammlung von Bordeaux-Jahrgängen ...

Background Information

Despite the hubris of British football fans, strong traces of traditional English »Bescheidenheit« are still present in society, and even **in business**. When Archie talks about his »modest country seat« he is referring, in **typically modest fashion**, to his rural home – which, you can be sure, is in reality a very fine house and grounds. And his wine cellar is sure to be stunning with a collection of Bordeaux vintages that can hardly be called »small«. *Rather* proud of it? He's sure to be very proud!

Train Yourself

Archie tells Peter that if he ever *finds himself* in Buckinghamshire he is a welcome guest. **In the following sentences replace the words in italics with expressions employing »find«:**

1. If he ever *discovers* that I tricked him into signing that contract I'll be in serious trouble.

....

2. Did you visit your aunt in hospital. How did you *think she looked?*

....

3. I just don't know how you *have* the time to keep up a job, a family and still study.

....

4. I *experience* much pleasure in following this particular course of study.

....

5. He is a very accomplished marksman. He *hits* the mark every time.

....

6. After a very long and complicated trial, the jury *pronounced* him guilty.

....

7. The archaeologists made a highly important *discovery* during their excavations in Syria.

....

8. We examined his personnel file and could *detect no reason* to criticize his performance.

....

Talk Talk Talk

P. Archie, did I tell you that my company is also **marketing** software providing for security in **online banking transactions**? We've had quite a bit of **success** with it.

P. Archie, habe ich Ihnen eigentlich erzählt, dass meine Firma auch Software für sichere **Banktransaktionen** über das **Internet auf den Markt bringt**? Wir haben damit einigen **Erfolg** gehabt.

A-S. I think you mentioned it, but my attention was on something else at the time. But you **develop** and market quite **a large range of products**, don't you? You must have a **large management staff** and **work force**.

A-S. Ich glaube, Sie haben es erwähnt, aber ich war damals etwas abgelenkt. Aber Sie **entwickeln** und vermarkten **eine ziemlich breite Palette an Produkten**, nicht wahr? Sie müssen ein **personalstarkes Management** und **viele Mitarbeiter** haben.

P. Surprisingly small, Archie. Management consists basically of our **managing director** and myself. We have a large **sales network** but only one of our people in London **specializes in** sales. Probably that's the success of our company.

P. Überraschend wenig, Archie. Das Management besteht im Wesentlichen aus unserem **Geschäftsführer** und mir selbst. Wir haben ein breites **Distributionsnetz**, aber nur einer unserer Leute in London ist tatsächlich auf den Verkauf **spezialisiert**. Vielleicht ist das der Erfolg unseres Unternehmens.

A-S. Good heavens, you're certainly **labour-intensive**. I imagine the company is highly **profitable**.

A-S. Meine Güte, das ist ja wirklich **arbeitsaufwendig**. Ich vermute, die Firma ist sehr **profitabel**.

P. Profitable, yes. But Ergo has an **ambitious expansion programme**. That's one of the reasons I'm here in New York. We would like to **pen-**

P. Profitabel schon. Aber Ergo betreibt auch ein **ehrgeiziges Expansionsprogramm**. Das ist einer der Gründe, warum ich hier

etrate the American market.

in New York bin. Wir würden gern **in den amerikanischen Markt vordringen**.

A-S. **Are you stock exchange-listed?**

A-S. **Seid ihr börsennotiert?**

P. Not yet, Archie. We're **preparing for a public share issue**, though, and I'm looking forward to it. It will give the company new **impetus**.

P. Noch nicht, Archie. Wir **bereiten uns auf eine Aktienemission vor** und ich freue mich darauf. Es wird der Firma neue **Schubkraft** bringen.

Train Yourself

Peter tells Archie he's looking forward to Ergo's appearance on the stock exchange – meaning he anticipates it with pleasure and interest. We have already looked at some common uses of the verb and noun »look«. Let's look now at some more – **replace the words in italics in the following sentences with expressions employing »look«:**

1. They could see very well what was happening but they chose *to ignore it*.

....

2. *Be careful!* You nearly collided with that bus.

....

3. Can you *take care of* the shop for me while I visit the hospital?

....

4. He treats his junior staff dreadfully, he *views them with utter disdain.*

....

5. We called the police and they promised to *examine* the case.

....

6. Givenchy has introduced a completely new *style* to women's fashion.

....

7. I am *relying on* you to show me how to do this work.

....

8. *Cheer up!* Things aren't that bad. In fact, business is *improving*.

....

Talk Talk Talk

A-S. How old is the company?

A-S. Seit wann besteht die Firma?

P. Ergo **was founded** some years ago, at the height of the **IT boom**. I gather the company started quite small, in **premises** outside London. The company moved its **headquarters** later to central London because it got a very good rental deal and it's a **prestigious** address. From there we've **extended** into Wales and now Scotland.

P. Ergo **wurde** vor ein paar Jahren **gegründet**, auf dem Höhepunkt des **IT-Booms**. Soweit ich weiß, hat die Firma ziemlich klein angefangen, in **Räumlichkeiten** außerhalb von London. Später hat sie ihr **Hauptquartier** ins Zentrum von London verlegt, weil sie gute Mietkonditionen für eine **angesehene** Adresse erhalten hat. Von da aus haben wir nach Wales und nun nach Schottland **expandiert**.

A-S. Ah yes, Glasgow. Is there somebody **minding the shop** up there while you're away?

A-S. Ah ja, Glasgow. **Kümmert sich jemand um das Geschäft,** während Sie unterwegs sind?

P. Oh yes, the advantage of having a small staff is that you're very **flexible**. I've had to **wear various hats** during my time with Ergo.

P. Oh ja, der Vorteil einer kleinen Belegschaft ist, dass man sehr **flexibel** ist. Ich musste während meiner Zeit bei Ergo schon viele **verschiedene Aufgaben übernehmen**.

A-S. Certainly different from my **set-up**. Banking is very compartmentalized, even the IT side of it.

A-S. Das ist ganz anders als mein **Arbeitshintergrund**. Das Bankgeschäft ist sehr aufgesplittert, auch auf der IT-Seite.

P. And is your company a product of the IT boom?

P. Und ist Ihre Firma auch ein Produkt des IT-Booms?

A-S. I suppose you could say so.

A-S. Ich denke, das könnte man so

The Royal Scottish and the Star banks **amalgamated** several years ago, but I **set up** my own **company** within the group in order to **meet the demands** of **increased security in online business**.

sagen. Die Royal Scottish Bank und die Star Banks haben vor ein paar Jahren **fusioniert**, aber ich habe innerhalb der Gruppe meine eigene **Firma gegründet**, um der **gesteigerten Nachfrage** nach **Sicherheit im Online-Business nachzukommen**.

P. And it appears to **be** very **successful** ...

P. Und Sie scheinen damit sehr **erfolgreich** zu **sein** ...

A-S. We**'re** not yet **in profit**, though. The banks are **making record profits** but we had to **invest** so **heavily in new technology** that it will still be at least three years before we **break even**.

A-S. Wir **sind** trotzdem noch nicht **in der Profitzone**. Die Banken **machen gewaltige Gewinne**, aber wir mussten so **viel in die Neue Technologie investieren**, dass es noch mindestens drei Jahre dauern wird, bis wir den **»Break-Even-Point« erreicht** haben.

Train Yourself

Let's revise the use of »someone«, »somebody«, »anyone«, »anybody«, »no one« and »nobody«. There are subtle differences, remember. Generally speaking, someone and somebody are used as singular pronouns, anyone and anybody as plural and indeterminate ones. »No-one« and »nobody« are the plural form of all four. **Select the correct form to use in the following sentences:**

1. There's ______ at the door. Shall I go?
2. Hello, is ______ there? Jack, I think there's ______ in the house.
3. I searched the place from top to bottom and found ______.
4. There's ______ here I know. I was expecting ______ to turn up.
5. Can't ______ fix your car for you? Is there ______ able to change a plug?

6. There's ______ coming up the hill now. I can see him quite clearly.

Background Information

Somebody is also used as a noun to describe a person of rank or importance. »He's quite a somebody in his town.«

Talk Talk Talk

A-S. Nonetheless, Peter, I do have enough **small change** in my pocket for a visit to a neighbouring bar, where some old friends are waiting for us.

A-S. Nichtsdestotrotz, Peter, habe ich genug **Kleingeld** in der Tasche, um einen Abstecher in die nächste Bar zu machen, wo ein paar alte Freunde schon auf uns warten.

P. I'm very tired, Archie ...

P. Ich bin sehr müde, Archie ...

AS. Nonsense. It's just a short taxi ride away ... Here we are, let's **check it out** ... Here are some of the people who have been waiting for you. Amanda! How nice of you to come.

AS. Unsinn. Es ist nur eine kurze Taxifahrt entfernt ... Da sind wir schon, **schauen wir mal** ... Hier sind ein paar Leute, die schon auf Sie gewartet haben. Amanda! Wie nett, dass Sie gekommen sind.

P. Don! Fancy meeting you here. And Rory. Is this your club or something?

P. Don! Was für ein Zufall Sie hier zu treffen. Und Rory. Ist das Ihr Club oder so?

D. It is tonight, Peter.

D. Heute Nacht ja, Peter.

A-S. They've all come to say good-bye to you, Peter.

A-S. Sie sind alle gekommen, um Ihnen Lebewohl zu sagen, Peter.

P. Well, what a surprise! What a send-off!

P. Na, was für eine Überraschung! Was für eine Verabschiedung!

A-S. You didn't think we were going to let you slip out of the country unnoticed, do you?

A-S. Sie haben doch nicht geglaubt, dass wir Sie so unbemerkt aus dem Land entkommen lassen, oder?

P. But why the TV cameras?

P. Aber warum die Fernsehkameras?

A-S. It's Amanda's **crew**. She has a new show, something like »Out and About in Manhattan«. She wants to do a piece on this party.

A-S. Das ist Amandas **Mannschaft**. Sie hat eine neue Show, so was wie »Out and About in Manhattan«. Sie möchte einen Beitrag über diese Party machen.

P. Did you **organize** this, Archie?

P. Haben Sie das **organisiert**, Archie?

A-S. Didn't I ever tell you I **was in marketing** for a while? If you want to **market your product** you market yourself first. First rule in marketing, you know ...

A-S. Habe ich Ihnen nie erzählt, dass ich eine Zeit lang **im Marketing war**? Wenn du **dein Produkt vermarkten** willst, vermarkte erst dich selbst. Die erste Regel im Marketing, wissen Sie ...

Background Information

Archie's right. His company clearly makes a very **good product**, but it's the force of his personality alone which has won its exposure to a wider market on American TV. That and his proven ability to **»network«**, to make easy and rapid **contact** with other people.

Train Yourself

Archie and Peter check out the Yellow Balloon bar, meaning they inspect it. **Check out the following sentences and insert the correct preposition in expressions using the word »check«:**

1. What time do we have to check __________ for our flight to London?
2. Could you check my car __________ today, please. Don't forget to check __________ the oil.
3. Is that the reception desk? What time do I have to check __________ by, please?
4. Can you go through this list of items and check __________ each one as you find it.
5. I checked __________ the accounts and found them to be correct.
6. Doctor, the patient is in West Ward. Could you find the time to check __________ her condition.
7. I'm rather doubtful about that man's credentials. Can you check __________ them, please.
8. This looks like a good hotel. Shall I check it __________ for us?

The possibilities: *on, up, through, out, up on, in, off*

Talk Talk Talk

Amanda: We'll miss you, you know, Peter. And I shall miss you most of all.

Amanda: Ehrlich, Peter, wir werden Sie vermissen. Und ich werde Sie von allen am meisten vermissen.

P. And I shall miss you all, Amanda. I really have enjoyed my stay in New York, and I have to thank you and everyone else here. You have done your best to make me feel at home and to have a good time.

P. Und ich werde Sie alle vermissen, Amanda. Ich habe meinen Aufenthalt in New York wirklich genossen und ich muss Ihnen und allen anderen hier danken. Sie haben Ihr Bestes gegeben, damit ich mich wie zu Hause fühle und eine schöne Zeit habe.

A-S. This calls for a toast. Fill your glasses, everybody. Are we all here?

A-S. Das ruft nach einem Trinkspruch. Alle Mann die Gläser füllen. Sind alle da?

Peter, **here's to you**, a safe return to London and **your continued success at Ergo**.

Peter, **auf Sie**, eine sichere Rückkehr nach London und **Ihren weiteren Erfolg bei Ergo.**

P. And here's to my new friends in New York – and to you Archie. I'll be back, I promise. This has given me a taste for America, I can tell you.

P. Und auf meine neuen Freunde in New York – und auf Sie, Archie. Ich komme zurück, versprochen. Bezüglich Amerika bin ich auf den Geschmack gekommen, das kann ich Ihnen sagen.

Rory: Next time, venture West. That's where the real America is to be found.

Rory: Wagen Sie sich das nächste Mal nach Westen. Dort kann man das wahre Amerika finden.

Don: Don't listen to him, Peter. Rory's a country boy, through and through. City life makes him uncomfortable.

Don: Hören Sie nicht auf ihn, Peter. Rory ist durch und durch ein Junge vom Land. Im Stadtleben fühlt er sich unwohl.

A. Good heavens, look who's here! I thought you were in Los Angeles.

A. Lieber Himmel, wen haben wir denn da? Ich dachte, du wärst in Los Angeles.

Troy Everett: Like you, Amanda, I don't like to miss a good party. And I'm also here in a **professional capacity**.

Troy Everett: Ebenso wie du, Amanda, verpasse ich nicht gerne eine gute Party. Und ich bin auch in meiner **beruflichen Eigenschaft** hier.

A. That sounds interesting.

A. Das hört sich interessant an.

Troy Everett: It sure is, Amanda. This here is James Duvall, from Columbia Pictures. They're making a costume drama set in Merry Old England. I told him about Archie, and he asked to meet him. Well,

Troy Everett: Das ist es mit Sicherheit, Amanda. Dies hier ist James Duvall von Columbia Pictures. Die machen gerade einen Kostümfilm, der im guten alten England spielt. Ich habe ihm von Archie erzählt

here we are ...

und er bat darum, ihn kennen zu lernen. Nun, hier sind wir ...

Train Yourself

Peter tells his friends at his farewell party that they have done their best to make him at home in New York. There are several common expressions using the word »best« – **complete the gaps in the following sentences with the right ones:**

1. If you want to get on in this company you'll have to put ____________ ____________.
2. John chose his brother to be ____________ at the wedding.
3. I know it's a disappointment, but try to put ____________ on it.
4. The very ____________ scenario is still quite bleak.
5. That holiday took up ____________ my savings. In fact, it left me nearly broke.
6. The first edition of his book was sold out within weeks. It has become a sensational ____________.

Talk Talk Talk

(Grand Hotel, reception)

(Grand Hotel, Rezeption)

P. Good morning, could I have my **bill**, please? Thank you. Does this **include service and taxes**?

P. Guten Morgen, könnte ich bitte meine **Rechnung** haben? Danke sehr. Ist sie **inklusive Service und Steuern**?

Receptionist. Yes sir. That's seven nights at 160 dollars a night, plus service and tax. And **your credit card charges** in the bar and restaurant. Did you have anything from the minibar since last night?

Empfangsdame: Ja, mein Herr. Das sind sieben Nächte zu 160 Dollar die Nacht plus Service und Steuern. Und Ihre **Kreditkartenbeträge** in der Bar und im Restaurant. Hatten Sie seit letzter Nacht irgendetwas aus der Minibar?

P. No, I'd drunk enough before coming back to the hotel! Could you get me a taxi to take me to the airport?

P. Nein, ich hatte genug getrunken, bevor ich ins Hotel zurückkam! Könnten Sie mir ein Taxi besorgen, das mich zum Flughafen bringt?

R. We can offer you the hotel limousine service at a very **favourable rate**. It will probably cost less than a taxi, and it's certainly more comfortable. When is your flight?

R. Wir können Ihnen den Hotel-limousinen-Service zu einem **Vorzugspreis** anbieten. Das wird Sie wahrscheinlich weniger als ein Taxi kosten und ist sicherlich komfortabler. Wann geht Ihr Flieger?

P. Eleven forty.

P. Elf Uhr vierzig.

R. Then **may I suggest** we reserve the limousine for you for nine thirty. That will give you plenty of time. Have you had breakfast?

R. **Darf ich** dann **vorschlagen**, dass wir die Limousine für neun Uhr dreißig für Sie reservieren. So haben Sie eine Menge Zeit. Haben Sie schon gefrühstückt?

P. No, I'm about to go to the breakfast room now.

P. Nein, ich gehe jetzt gleich ins Frühstückszimmer.

R. Then I'll call you when the limousine is here.

R. Dann werde ich Sie rufen, wenn die Limousine hier ist.

P. That's very kind of you. Thank you.

P. Das ist sehr nett von Ihnen. Danke sehr.

R. Don't mention it, sir. Have a nice day!

R. Nicht der Rede wert, mein Herr. Schönen Tag noch!

Background Information

»Have a nice day!« is a favourite **American farewell**. It has become so common that many people find it irritating, so avoid using it. A plain »Goodbye« is much preferable. »Ciao« is strictly for the Italians!

Train Yourself

The hotel offers Peter a limousine service to the airport at a very »favourable« rate – meaning, of course, at a charge likely to please him. The hotel hopes Peter will favour its limousine service, in contrast to the slower and less comfortable taxi ride. There are several everyday expressions based on the word »favour«. **Find the correct ones in the following sentences:**

1. The bank has told me my account has a balance ______ of more than two thousand dollars.
2. The jury returned a verdict ______ the accused.
3. That horse couldn't fail to win. The odds ______ were very high indeed.
4. The ruling party are very likely to lose the next election, they are seriously ______ with the general public.
5. The fine weather ______ our annual outing to the sea.
6. Could you please ______ and pass the salt?

Background Information

»Favour« is written »favor« in American English – a further example of the American tendency to simplify the language (although some experts say these »simplified« forms are remnants of early English). Other examples where American English drops that unnecessary »o« include: color, odor, parlor, rancor, rigor. A similar process can be seen in the American treatment of words with gallic endings, such as manoeuvre – which is simplied to »maneuver«.

Talk Talk Talk

(Breakfast room at the Grand Hotel)	(Frühstückszimmer im Grand Hotel)
P. Good heavens! Archie! What are you doing here. I thought you	P. Lieber Himmel! Archie! Was machen Sie hier. Ich dachte, Sie

would be sleeping off a heavy hangover.

würden Ihren gewaltigen Kater ausschlafen.

A-S. Peter, I couldn't let you slip off without saying a final farewell. Besides, I have this present for you.

A-S. Peter, Ich konnte Sie nicht abreisen lassen, ohne mich noch einmal ein letztes Mal von Ihnen zu verabschieden. Übrigens, ich habe ein Geschenk für Sie.

P. That's very kind. Will you join me for some breakfast, Archie?

P. Das ist sehr nett von Ihnen! Möchten Sie mit mir frühstücken, Archie?

A-S. Just some coffee, thank you. Well, Peter, what are the impressions you will be taking back with you? How do you find the American way of **doing business**?

A-S. Nur eine Tasse Kaffee, danke. Also, Peter, was für Eindrücke werden Sie mit nach Hause nehmen? Was halten Sie von der amerikanischen Art, **Geschäfte zu machen**?

P. I was surprised, I must say, at the amount of business which is conducted in relatively informal surroundings – restaurants, even in bars.

P. Ich muss ganz ehrlich zugeben, es hat mich überrascht, wie viele Geschäftsgespräche in informeller Umgebung stattfinden – wie etwa in Restaurants oder sogar Bars.

A-S. I'm used to it, of course. It's also a very English style, as you've already certainly discovered in London.

A-S. Ich bin natürlich daran gewöhnt. Wie Sie bestimmt schon in London gemerkt haben, ist dies auch eine sehr englische Art.

P. You're right. This informal manner of conducting often very important **business talks** has **struck** me there, too. It's scarcely the German way. I'm not saying either way is any better than the other.

P. Sie haben Recht. Diese doch sehr informelle Art, **Geschäftsgespräche** zu führen – oft auch sehr wichtige – ist mir schon dort **aufgefallen**. Sie entspricht kaum der deutschen Art. Ich will damit aber nicht sagen, dass die eine besser ist als die andere.

A-S. We certainly admire the correct German style, even though it sometimes doesn't match my own personal drinking and eating routine!

A-S. Wir bewundern die korrekte deutsche Arbeitsweise sehr, obwohl sie sich manchmal nicht mit meinen eigenen Ess- und Trinkgewohnheiten in Einklang bringen lässt!

P. Well, it's coffee for you this morning, Archie. Now, let me see what you've brought me. What have we here? A coffee pot. Archie, this must have **cost a bomb**. It's from a 19th century Chicago manufacturer. The kiln doesn't exist any more – this is a collector's piece.

P. Nun, heute Morgen gibt es nur Kaffee für Sie, Archie. Jetzt zeigen Sie mir doch einmal, was Sie mir mitgebracht haben. Einen Kaffeetopf. Archie, der muss ein **Vermögen gekostet** haben. Er ist aus einer Manufaktur aus dem Chicago des 19. Jahrhunderts. Der Brennofen existiert nicht mehr – das ist ein Sammlerstück.

A-S. I know, Peter. I thought you might like it. Amanda hunted it down. But, wait a minute, how come you know so much about early American pottery?

A-S. Ich weiß, Peter. Ich dachte, er würde Ihnen gefallen. Amanda hat ihn ausfindig gemacht. Aber, warten Sie mal, wieso wissen Sie so viel über frühe amerikanische Töpferwaren?

P. Archie, my grandfather was **founder** of a porcelain **factory** in Saxony. I used to warm my hands in winter at his furnace.

P. Archie, mein Großvater war der **Gründer** einer Porzellan**fabrik** in Sachsen. Ich habe mir im Winter immer die Hände an seinem Hochofen gewärmt.

A-S. Well, I never, Peter – you really are a man of many parts ...

A-S. Nicht zu fassen, Peter – Sie sind wirklich ein Mann mit vielen Facetten ...

Train Yourself

Archie uses a very colloquial expression when he asks Peter »how come« he knows so much about porcelain and pottery. There are others employing »come«. **Combine »come« with any of the words in italics at the end of the exercise to produce the correct expressions in the following sentences:**

1. Tell me the whole story of how that crime was committed/__________.
2. How did the speaker __________? Did he impress his audience?
3. She has made remarkable progress in the past three years. She is a fine example of how one can __________ one's own.
4. That story has __________ over the centuries. I never thought it was so old.
5. That politician has __________ for much criticism because of his broken promises.
6. When you look closely at that problem and __________ to its basic causes you can see that a solution will be hard to find.
7. Work on the new project is progressing well, it's __________ fine.
8. We need a leader, and that's where you __________.

The possibilities: *along, in, one, into, clean, down, across, down*

Vocabulary

to amalgamate	fusionieren, sich zusammenschließen
ambitious	ehrgeizig
annual holiday	Jahresurlaub
to be in marketing	im Marketing tätig sein
to be stock exchange-listed	börsennotiert sein
be my guest	bedienen Sie sich
to break even	den »Break-Even-Point« erreichen
business talks	Geschäftsgespräche
to care for	sich etwas machen aus
to check it out	unter die Lupe nehmen
to cost a bomb	ein Vermögen kosten
credit card charges	Kreditkartenbeträge
crew	Mannschaft
deal	Handel, Geschäft, Abmachung
to develop	entwickeln

to do business	Geschäfte machen
e-commerce	E-Commerce
expansion programme	Expansionsprogramm
to extend	expandieren
factory	Fabrik
favourable rate	Vorzugspreis
Fine by me!	Einverstanden!
flexible	flexibel
for free	umsonst
to found	gründen
founder	Gründer
to go into banking	sich dem Bankwesen widmen
headquarters	Hauptquartier
Here's to (you, us etc)!	Auf (Sie, uns, etc.)!
I do hope we stay in contact	ich hoffe, wir bleiben in Kontakt
I'd like to show you ...	ich würde Ihnen gerne ... zeigen
impetus	Schubkraft
service and taxes included	inklusive Service und Steuern
industrial actions	Arbeitskämpfe
to be in profit	in der Profitzone sein
to invest (heavily) in	(viel) investieren in
IT boom	IT-Boom
labour-intensive	arbeitsintensiv
large management staff	personalstarkes Management
large range of products	breite Palette an Produkten
to make record profits	gewaltige Gewinne machen
managing director	Managing Director, Geschäftsführer
to market a product	ein Produkt vermarkten
May I suggest ...?	Darf ich vorschlagen ...?
to meet the demands	der Nachfrage nachkommen
mobile	Mobiltelefon, Handy
network	Netz (Straßen, Kontakte, etc.)
to network	Geschäftsverbindungen aufbauen
new technology	Neue Technologie
to organize	organisieren
online banking	Onlinebanking
to penetrate a market	in einen Markt vordringen

premises	Räumlichkeiten, Büroräume
to prepare for	sich vorbereiten auf
prestigious	angesehen
professional capacity	berufliche Eigenschaft
profitable	Gewinn bringend
public share issue	Aktienemission
to put in the shade	in den Schatten stellen
to rise	steigen, ansteigen
sales network	Distributionsnetz
security in online business	Sicherheit im Online-Business
set up	Arbeitshintergrund
to set up a company	eine Firma gründen
small change	Kleingeld
to specialize in	sich spezialisieren auf einem Gebiet
strike	Streik
to strike somebody	jemandem auffallen
success	Erfolg
take over Ergo operations	die Geschäfte von Ergo übernehmen
transaction	Transaktion
union	Gewerkschaft
to wear various hats	verschiedene Aufgaben übernehmen
work force	Arbeitskräfte, hier: Mitarbeiter
working hours	Arbeitszeiten

Working conditions
Arbeitskonditionen

Here we go

Peter kehrt nach London zurück, wobei er auf dem Flug einen weiteren interessanten Mitreisenden kennen lernt – den Besitzer eines russischen Export-Import-Unternehmens. Zurück im Büro ist es seine erste Aufgabe, sich auf eine wichtige Konferenz vorzubereiten. Er ist froh, als er erfährt, dass er wieder mit Beryl zusammenarbeitet ...

Talk Talk Talk

(J.F. Kennedy Airport, New York)	(J.F. Kennedy Flughafen, New York)
Flight attendant: Good morning. Your boarding pass? 20 A. Down the right-hand aisle ...	Flugbegleiter: Guten Morgen. Ihre Boardingkarte? 20 A. Den rechten Gang hinunter ...
P. Oh, no. It's happened again. Somebody is in my seat. Excuse me, **I'm sorry to disturb you**, but you appear to be in my seat.	P. Oh nein. Es ist schon wieder geschehen. Jemand sitzt auf meinem Platz. Entschuldigen Sie, **es tut mir Leid, Sie zu stören**, aber Sie scheinen auf meinem Platz zu sitzen.
Fellow passenger: Oh, I am so sorry. This is 20 B, is it not?	Mitreisender: Oh, das tut mir sehr Leid. Ist das 20 B? Nein?
P. No, actually it's not. It's 20 A. This seat here is 20 B.	P. Nein, eigentlich nicht. Es ist 20 A. Dieser Platz hier ist 20 B.
FP. Oh, my sincere apologies. I shall move right away.	MR. Oh, ich entschuldige mich vielmals. Ich werde mich sofort umsetzen.

P. I'm sorry if I'm making a fuss about it, but I did specifically request a window seat. I'm like a child **when it comes to** flying. I do like to look out of the window – particularly when all New York is below us.

P. Es tut mir Leid, wenn ich deswegen Umstände mache, aber ich habe extra einen Fensterplatz verlangt. **Was** das Fliegen **betrifft**, bin ich wie ein Kind. Ich sehe gern aus dem Fenster – besonders wenn ganz New York unter uns liegt.

FP. Oh, I know. I also never get tired of looking at Moscow from the air.

MR. Oh, das verstehe ich. Ich werde auch niemals müde, Moskau aus der Luft zu betrachten.

P. You are from Moscow?

P. Sie sind aus Moskau?

FP. Yes, I am Russian, although I spend a lot of time in America. My two brothers are there, **in business**.

FP. Ja, ich bin Russe, obwohl ich viel Zeit in Amerika verbringe. Meine zwei Brüder sind dort **beruflich**.

P. And you visit them frequently?

P. Und Sie besuchen sie häufig?

FP. Oh, yes, as often as I can. And you? You are not American?! Judging by your accent, you must be from Europe. Correct?

FP. Aber ja, so oft ich kann. Und Sie? Sie sind kein Amerikaner?! Ihrem Akzent nach kommen Sie, denke ich, aus Europa. Oder?

P. Yes, you are right. I am German, although I am working in Britain at the moment. **Allow me to introduce myself.** Peter Brückner.

P. Ja, Sie haben Recht. Ich bin Deutscher, obwohl ich momentan in Großbritannien arbeite. **Erlauben Sie mir, mich vorzustellen.** Peter Brückner.

FP. And I am Sergei Fedorov. At your service.

FP. Und ich bin Sergei Fedorov. Sehr erfreut.

P. **I'm very pleased to meet you.** Oh, here we go, I'm always a bit nervous at takeoff ...

P. **Ich freue mich, Ihre Bekanntschaft zu machen**. Oh, es geht los. Ich bin immer ein bisschen nervös beim Start ...

Train Yourself

Peter's new acquaintance, Sergei Fedorov, speaks good English but nevertheless makes some of the errors typical for Russian speakers. **Can you detect them?** A clue – they have to do with his use of the verb »to move«, »to grow tired«, his use of some prepositions, adjectives, forms of speech – and the definite or indefinite article.

....

....

....

....

....

Background Information

As Peter's encounter with a Russian traveller shows, even a misunderstanding can afford the opportunity to **develop an interesting acquaintance**. Diplomacy in even the most difficult situations has its own rewards!

Talk Talk Talk

P. So, are you on your way back to Moscow by way of London?	P. Also, führt Sie der Rückweg nach Moskau über London?
SF. No. I have to travel to Berlin. I shall stay in London for five days, then I fly on to Berlin.	SF. Nein, ich muss nach Berlin reisen. Ich bleibe fünf Tage in London, dann fliege ich weiter nach Berlin.
P. And **what do you do, if I may ask?**	P. Und **was machen Sie, wenn ich fragen darf?**

SF. I **run** an **import-export business**.

SF. Ich **leite** ein **Import-Export-Unternehmen**.

P. Do you **specialize** in any particular products?

P. Sind Sie auf irgendwelche bestimmten Produkte **spezialisiert**?

SF. Mostly **high-tech** – computers, **software** and so on.

SF. Vor allem **Hightech** – Computer, **Software** und so weiter.

P. How very interesting. **That's my area of business, too.** Do the Russians have anything new to offer in that **line**?

P. Höchst interessant. **Das ist auch mein Geschäftsgebiet.** Haben die Russen in dieser **Branche** irgendetwas Neues anzubieten?

SF. Line? Oh, you mean in high-tech? Yes, certainly. We were far behind, but we are **catching up** very quickly and there are some areas where we may even be ahead.

SF. Branche? Oh, Sie meinen in Hightech? Ja natürlich. Wir waren weit zurück, aber wir **holen** schnell **auf** und es gibt ein paar Gebiete, wo wir vielleicht sogar vorn liegen.

P. That is most interesting to hear. I think we have a very interesting journey ahead of us both ...

P. Höchst interessant, das zu hören. Ich denke, wir haben beide eine sehr interessante Reise vor uns ...

Train Yourself

Peter asks Fedorov if he is on his way back to Moscow. **In the following sentences substitute the words and expressions in italics with ones using »way«:**

1. They deliberately planted those trees *in such a fashion that would hinder traffic.*

....

2. John *gets along very well with people*.

....

3. Watch Jane's career, she's *progressing well.*

4. I'm no marksman. I *missed the target by miles!*

5. *Incidentally,* why did you even bother applying for that job?

6. *He completed the job* and then went to the soccer match.

Talk Talk Talk

Cockpit announcement: Good afternoon again, ladies and gentlemen. We shall shortly be landing at Heathrow Airport, where the local time is nine ten in the evening. Visibility is good and the ground temperature is 10 degrees Celsius. Please now fasten your seatbelts, put your seats in an upright position and prepare for landing. We hope you have had a pleasant flight and look forward to having you aboard again.

Pilotendurchsage: Nochmals einen schönen Nachmittag, meine Damen und Herren. Wir werden in Kürze auf dem Flughafen Heathrow landen, wo die Ortszeit einundzwanzig Uhr zehn beträgt. Die Sicht ist gut und die Bodentemperatur beträgt 10 Grad Celsius. Bitte schließen Sie jetzt ihre Sicherheitsgurte, bringen Sie Ihre Sitze in eine aufrechte Position und machen Sie sich bereit für die Landung. Wir hoffen, Sie hatten einen angenehmen Flug und würden uns freuen, Sie bald wieder an Bord begrüßen zu können.

P. Well, that was a quick flight. Probably because I had you for company, Sergei – I may now call you Sergei, I hope?

P. Nun, das war ein kurzer Flug. Wahrscheinlich, weil ich Sie zur Gesellschaft hatte, Sergei – ich hoffe, ich darf Sie jetzt Sergei nennen?

F. Certainly, Peter. **Here is my card.** If you are ever in Moscow please call me. And thank you most kindly for all the information you gave me about Berlin.

F. Natürlich, Peter. **Hier ist meine Karte.** Wenn Sie irgendwann in Moskau sind, rufen Sie mich bitte an. Und herzlichen Dank für die ganzen Informationen, die Sie mir über Berlin gegeben haben.

P. It was a pleasure, Sergei. You have certainly given me much **information** about new **markets**.

P. Es war mir ein Vergnügen, Sergei. Sie haben mir auf alle Fälle viele **Informationen** über neue **Märkte** gegeben.

Train Yourself

The captain tells passengers the aircraft will shortly be landing at Heathrow – meaning the plane will soon be touching down. **In the following sentences combine the word »short« with any (or none) of the words in parantheses to replace the words and expressions in italics:**

1. The flight from London to Manchester is *very brief.*

2. Our business plan is *one which only covers the next few months.*

3. This instruction has to be carried out *very quickly indeed.*

4. We completed that order *with far less people than planned.*

5. The company *put together the names of the candidates most likely to get the job.*

6. They *lacked foresight* in not taking the present crisis into account.

7. If the company carries on like this it is likely to *go under very soon.*

(*range, handed, haul, sighted, listed, lived, changed, order, form, term*)

Talk Talk Talk

(Heathrow Airport; currency exchange counter)

(Flughafen Heathrow; Geldwechselschalter)

P. Good evening, I'd like to change these dollars back into sterling, please.

P. Guten Abend. Ich würde gerne diese Dollars in Pfund umtauschen.

Clerk: Certainly, sir. There is a one per cent **commission charge**, minimum three pounds. Is that all right?

Angestellter: Natürlich, mein Herr. Das macht ein Prozent **Provision**, Minimum drei Pfund. Ist das in Ordnung?

P. Yes, I suppose so. I need the money to get into central London.

P. Ja, ich denke schon. Ich brauche das Geld, um ins Zentrum Londons zu kommen.

Clerk: Here we are then. That makes forty pounds.

Angestellter: Alles klar. Das macht vierzig Pfund.

P. Where can I get the underground into central London?

P. Wie komme ich zur U-Bahn in Richtung London Zentrum?

Clerk: To your left and straight on. You can't miss it. The entrance is well marked ...

Angestellter: Nach links und geradeaus. Sie können es nicht verfehlen. Der Eingang ist gut beschildert ...

(Peter's flat; telephone rings)

(Peters Wohnung; das Telefon klingelt)

P. Hello, Peter Brückner here.

P. Hallo, hier spricht Peter

Melissa! How nice to hear from you. Where are you?

Brückner. Melissa! Wie schön, von Ihnen zu hören. Wo sind Sie?

M. I'm in Los Angeles. I tried to call you before you left, just to wish you a safe journey back. But you were never in your hotel, and I was very **busy** here.

M. Ich bin in Los Angeles. Ich habe versucht, Sie vor Ihrer Rückkehr noch anzurufen, um Ihnen eine gute Reise zu wünschen. Aber Sie waren nie in Ihrem Hotel und ich war hier sehr **beschäftigt**.

P. Los Angeles! What are you doing there?

P. Los Angeles! Was machen Sie denn dort?

M. I'm **chasing** a big account. The pace here is quite different from Britain. I can hardly **keep up** – it's New York one day, Chicago the next and then Los Angeles.

M. Ich bin **hinter** einem großen Auftrag **her**. Das Tempo hier unterscheidet sich ziemlich von Großbritannien. Ich kann kaum **mithalten** – einen Tag ist es New York, am nächsten Chicago und dann Los Angeles.

P. But you sound happy enough.

P. Aber Sie hören sich ganz glücklich an.

M. Well, **the work's fine**, but I miss Edinburgh – and, of course, London.

M. Na ja, **die Arbeit läuft gut**, aber ich vermisse Edinburgh – und natürlich London.

P. Funnily enough, so did I, in just my few days in New York. It's good to be home again.

P. Ich witzigerweise auch während meiner wenigen Tage in New York. Es tut gut, wieder zu Hause zu sein.

M. It's nice to hear you call London home. When are you going back to Glasgow?

M. Schön zu hören, dass Sie London Ihr Zuhause nennen. Wann gehen Sie zurück nach Glasgow?

P. I guess I'll find out tomorrow

P. Ich nehme an, das werde ich

when I get to the office ...	herausfinden, wenn ich morgen ins Büro komme ...

Background Information

Peter is told by the clerk at the currency exchange office that his dollars **»make«** forty pounds, meaning that's the amount of sterling he gets for his American cash. That use of the verb »make« is straightforward – but others are not so easy. Consider these:

to make do	to manage with the means in hand
to make light of	to play down the importance of something, to treat it as of little consequence
to make off	to go away
to make off/away with	to steal
to make out	to see or discern with difficulty; to get along
to make public	to disclose publicly
to make up	to invent, to concoct (a story, an account); to put together; to compensate
to make waves	to create a stir or disturbance

Train Yourself

Replace the words and expressions in italics in the following sentences with ones using forms of »make«:

1. The fog is so thick I can hardly *see* the lights of the city.

....

2. It's a mystery to me how they can *manage* with so little money.

....

3. Don't believe a word – all his stories are *concocted.*

4. That was a very serious matter, even though they *treated it lightly.*

5. Her stage debut *created quite a stir.*

6. If I were you, I'd *get out of here* as quickly as possible.

7. The burglars who broke into the manor house *stole* a number of valuable paintings.

8. The company has finally *disclosed* the full extent of its financial woes.

Talk Talk Talk

(Ergo offices, London)

Lucy: Mr Brückner! Peter! You're back! How lovely to see you again. Did you have a good flight? How was New York? Did you see Miss Walker there? She called here for your address, you know. Oh, I have so many questions, but you'll be wanting to speak to Mr Morgan. Come along please ... Mr Morgan – Peter, Mr Brückner, is back. Isn't it lovely to have him back with us again? I'll pop off and get you both a nice pot of tea. You'll have a lot

(Ergo-Büros, London)

Lucy: Mr Brückner! Peter! Sie sind zurück! Wie schön, Sie wieder zu sehen. Hatten Sie einen guten Flug? Wie war es in New York? Haben Sie dort Miss Walker gesehen? Sie hat hier wegen Ihrer Adresse angerufen, wissen Sie. Oh, ich habe so viele Fragen, aber Sie werden mit Mr Morgan sprechen wollen. Kommen Sie bitte mit ... Mr Morgan – Peter, Mr Brückner, ist zurück. Ist es nicht wunderbar, ihn wieder bei uns zu haben?

to talk about. A proper chin-wag, **I'll be bound** ...

Ich werde schnell verschwinden und Ihnen beiden eine schöne Kanne Tee holen. Sie werden viel zu besprechen haben. Einen ordentlichen Schwatz, da **bin ich sicher** ...

James Morgan: Peter, how are you? Good to see you again. Do sit down, and tell me all about New York. How did you find the **Ergo operation** there?

James Morgan: Peter, wie geht es Ihnen? Schön, Sie wieder zu sehen. Setzen Sie sich doch und erzählen Sie mir alles über New York. Wie fanden Sie dort die **Geschäfte von Ergo**?

P. I'm sure it's **in very good hands**. Don is very **experienced** and professional in his work. In addition, he did **everything in his power** to make me feel at home and get to know the operation. I think we're in a **strong position** and ready for **expansion** further into America.

P. Ich bin sicher, sie sind **in sehr guten Händen**. Don ist sehr **routiniert** und professionell in seiner Arbeit. Zudem hat er **alles in seiner Macht Stehende** getan, damit ich mich wie zu Hause fühle und das Geschäft kennen lerne. Ich denke, wir sind in einer **starken Position** und für eine weitere **Expansion** in Amerika bereit.

J. That's good to hear. I have that impression, too. Did you like New York?

J. Gut, das zu hören. Ich habe auch diesen Eindruck. Hat es Ihnen in New York gefallen?

P. Very much. Of course, quite different to London. I found New York is a very pulsating and exciting city. I'm glad to be back in London, though.

P. Sehr. Es ist natürlich ganz anders als London. New York ist für mich eine sehr pulsierende und aufregende Stadt. Trotzdem bin ich froh, zurück in London zu sein.

J. Not for long, Peter. We still need you in Glasgow. But take your time to settle back into **routine**. I have

J. Nicht für lange, Peter. Wir brauchen Sie immer noch in Glasgow. Aber nehmen Sie sich

an important **conference** for you to **attend** next week ...	Zeit, wieder zur **Routine** zurückzukehren. Nächste Woche müssen Sie an einer wichtigen **Konferenz teilnehmen** ...

Background Information

Peter tells James Morgan he believes Ergo Limited is in **»good hands«** in New York – meaning he believes the company is being managed well there. There are several everyday expressions using the simple word **»hand«** – including:

at hand	within reach
at the hands of	by or through the action of somebody or something
to hand down	to pass on from hand to hand (as from father to son); to deliver a judgment or sentence
to hand in	to submit, to deliver
Hands off!	Don't touch!
to hand over	to surrender, to give up
on hand	readily available
out of hand	without delay or deliberation; uncontrolled or uncontrollable

Train Yourself

In the following sentences, replace the words and expressions in italics with forms using »hand«:

1. *Don't touch* those shelves – they contain priceless porcelain.

....

2. Most of the company's aims are now *within reach.*

....

3. This ancient bible has been *passed on* from generation to generation of my family.

....

4. After you've completed these forms please *submit them* to the registrar.

....

5. The enemy troops *gave up* their stronghold without a fight.

....

6. The judge *administered* a very severe sentence in that embezzlement case.

....

7. The national soccer side suffered a punishing defeat *by the* Brazilian eleven.

....

8. I have all the ingredients for tonight's meal *readily available.*

....

9. The company dismissed their complaint *summarily and without deliberation.*

....

10. The neighbour's children are very badly behaved, they've got quite *out of control.*

....

Talk Talk Talk

P. Beryl! How are you? I haven't seen you for so long! You're looking great. As young as ever! Are you still **organizing press conferences**?

P. Beryl! Wie geht es Ihnen? Ich habe Sie so lange nicht gesehen! Sie sehen großartig aus. Jung wie immer! **Organisieren** Sie immer noch **Pressekonferenzen**?

B. Mr Morgan has **put me in charge of promotion** and **conferencing**. I'm organizing your participation at next week's one. I'm so glad to see you again, Mr Brückner. How was Glasgow, and how was New York?

B. Mr Morgan hat mir die **Verantwortung** für **Promotion** und **Konferenzen übertragen**. Ich organisiere Ihre Teilnahme an der Konferenz nächste Woche. Ich freue mich so, Sie wieder zu sehen, Mr Brückner. Wie war es in Glasgow, und wie war es in New York?

P. Beryl, it would take all day to tell you, and I know you have a hundred and one things to do. But, tell me, how is your nephew **getting along**? Did he **start** as planned **with the company**?

P. Beryl, es würde den ganzen Tag dauern, Ihnen das zu erzählen, und ich weiß, Sie haben sehr viele Dinge zu erledigen. Aber sagen Sie mir, wie **kommt** Ihr Neffe **zurecht**? Hat er wie geplant **bei der Firma angefangen**?

B. Oh yes. He's joined the **sales staff** under Steve and doing ever so well.

B. Oh ja. Er ist in der Abteilung von Steve beim **Verkaufspersonal** und macht sich sehr gut.

P. I'm glad to hear it. Steve is a very good boss.

P. Freut mich zu hören. Steve ist ein sehr guter Chef.

B. We have to **organize a meeting** some time in the next few days to **discuss the conference**. Mr Morgan says it will be an ideal opportunity to **widen our circle of contacts**. **Networking**, he calls it.

B. Wir müssen irgendwann in den nächsten Tagen **ein Treffen organisieren**, um die **Konferenz zu besprechen**. Mr Morgan meint, es wird eine ausgezeichnete Gelegenheit sein, unseren **Kreis an Kontakten zu erweitern**. Er nennt das **Networking**.

P. That's something I picked up in New York. The Americans are very good at it, even though their style is sometimes a bit unconventional.

P. Das ist etwas, das ich in New York aufgeschnappt habe. Die Amerikaner sind sehr gut darin, obwohl ihre Art manchmal ein wenig ungewöhnlich ist.

B. I've never been to America. London's big enough for me at the moment.

B. Ich war noch nie in Amerika. London ist im Augenblick groß genug für mich.

P. London is getting to know you. This conferencing job gets you to meet a lot of people, I imagine?

P. Sie werden ja noch in ganz London bekannt. Ich kann mir vorstellen, dass Sie bei dieser Konferenztätigkeit eine Menge Leute kennen lernen.

B. Oh, yes! I even met my future husband at an **electronics symposium**.

B. Oh ja! Ich habe sogar meinen zukünftigen Ehemann bei einem **Elektronik-Symposium** kennen gelernt.

P. Your future husband? Beryl! You're a fast worker. You certainly don't let the grass grow under your feet. Does that mean I've lost you now?

P. Ihren zukünftigen Ehemann? Beryl! Sie sind eine emsige Biene. Sie lassen wohl nichts anbrennen. Bedeutet das jetzt, dass ich Sie verloren habe?

B. Oh, Mr Brückner. You know your heart's elsewhere.

B. Oh, Mr Brückner. Sie wissen, Ihr Herz ist anderswo.

P. Yes, in my work right now, Beryl. So let's **get down to it**. When's the wedding, by the way? I hope it doesn't interfere with our **schedule** ...

P. Ja Beryl, jetzt gerade bei meiner Arbeit. Also fangen wir an. Übrigens, wann ist die Hochzeit? Ich hoffe, sie überschneidet sich nicht mit unserem **Terminkalender** ...

Background Information

»Conferencing« – the organization of **conferences** – is becoming big business, particularly exploiting the new opportunities being opened up in **electronic communications**. Companies are increasingly turning to **»virtual conferences«**, where participants are brought together electronically, communicating with each other via the

internet and **on-screen video link-ups**. Ergo Limited isn't at that stage yet, but it still employs Beryl full time on keeping in touch with the conference circuit and even organizing the company's own theme-specific conferences – conferencing.

Background Information

Peter tells Beryl ironically that London **is getting to know her** – meaning she is becoming known in the city. »Get to« has the meaning of »beginning«, »starting on something«:
»I'm getting to like living here«; »I'll get to that job of work as soon as I can«; »When do I get to drive the car?«
We've already looked at several expressions using the verb **»get«**.
Here are some more:

to get a bead on	to acquire knowledge of something
to get after	to pursue energetically
to get a move on	to hurry
to get away with	to avoid discovery, reprimand or punishment
to get cracking	to start out, to start on something
to get even with	to avenge oneself
to get somewhere	to succeed, to make progress
to get wind of	to become aware of something

Train Yourself

Now complete the following sentences using any of the above expressions with »get«:

1. She has become superintendant of the regional hospital. I always knew that girl would ______.
2. It's very late, the sun is up. If we want to get there by this evening it's time to ______.

3. If you __________ them now you might catch them before they do any more harm.
4. When they told me John was leaving the company I wasn't surprised. I'd __________ his dissatisfaction some time ago.
5. Can you try and __________ this vital piece of information?
6. Oh, come on __________. At this rate, we'll never get there.
7. The jury returned a not guilty verdict, although I thought he'd never __________.
8. I have resolved __________ for the way she treated me.

Talk Talk Talk

J. What about a spot of lunch, Peter? You can then tell me all about your trip.

J. Wie wäre es mit einem Happen zu Essen, Peter? Sie können mir dann alles über Ihre Reise erzählen.

P. I'd like that, James. Where shall we go?

P. Gerne, James. Wohin sollen wir gehen?

J. Oh, the usual. Let's have a beer first at the Duke of York. Let's go! Lucy, be a dear and **take any messages**. We'll be back by two. If you go to lunch before then let Chip **take over**.

J. Ach, das Übliche. Lassen Sie uns zuerst ein Bier im Duke of York trinken. Gehen wir! Lucy, seien Sie so lieb und **nehmen Sie alle Nachrichten entgegen**. Wir werden gegen zwei Uhr zurück sein. Wenn Sie vorher zum Mittagessen gehen, soll Chip übernehmen.

L. I'm sending out for sandwiches, Mr Morgan. There's that much to do today.

L. Ich lasse mir Sandwiches kommen, Mr Morgan. Es ist heute so viel zu tun.

(Duke of York pub)

(Duke of York Pub)

J. Good girl, that Lucy. I don't know what we'd do without her. We've

J. Ein Goldstück, diese Lucy. Ich wüsste nicht, was wir ohne sie

got a good **team** together now, although we do miss Melissa.

machen würden. Wir haben jetzt ein gutes **Team** zusammen, obwohl wir Melissa vermissen.

P. So do I.

P. Das tue ich auch.

J. Oh, there's David Chatham, manager of our bank. He's just lost his father – died the other day from a stroke. David, I was very sorry to hear the news. Please accept my condolences.

J. Oh, da ist David Chatham, unser Bankmanager. Er hat gerade seinen Vater verloren – er verstarb vor kurzem an einem Schlaganfall. David, es tat mir sehr Leid, die Neuigkeiten zu hören. Bitte nehmen Sie mein Beileid entgegen.

D. Thank you, James. It was a shock to us all, I must admit. He had seemed so healthy. He was playing golf the day before the stroke.

D. Danke James. Ich muss gestehen, es war für uns alle ein Schock. Er hatte so gesund gewirkt. Am Tag vor dem Schlaganfall hat er Golf gespielt.

J. Please pass on my condolences to your wife. She was a very good daughter-in-law, I know – I have very good memories of the dinner parties she gave for your father.

J. Bitte richten Sie auch Ihrer Frau mein Beileid aus. Ich weiß, sie war eine sehr gute Schwiegertochter – ich erinnere mich sehr gut an die Dinnerparties, die sie für Ihren Vater gab.

D. I'll do that James.

D. Das werde ich tun, James.

J. David, meet my **assistant**, Peter Brückner. He's just back from New York.

J. David, darf ich Ihnen meinen **Stellvertreter** Peter Brückner vorstellen. Er ist gerade aus New York zurück.

D. **How do you do.** Are you American?

D. **Guten Tag.** Sind Sie Amerikaner?

P. Oh, no. Actually I'm German. I

P. Oh nein. Eigentlich bin ich

came here **on secondment** to Ergo, but now I think I'm here to stay – is that right, James?

Deutscher. Ich wurde zu Ergo **abgeordnet**, aber jetzt glaube ich, werde ich hier bleiben – nicht wahr, James?

J. I certainly hope so, Peter. I don't want to lose you ...

J. Das hoffe ich selbstverständlich, Peter. Ich möchte Sie nicht verlieren ...

Background Information

James Morgan's friend David Chatham has just lost his father – meaning his father has died. There are several everyday expressions using the verb **»lose«**:

to lose faith	to fail to believe any more in something
to lose heart	to become less enthusiastic
to lose one's heart	to fall in love
to lose one's temper	to fail to keep control of one's anger
to lose the initiative	to give up the leadership, to fall behind
to lose the sense of something, to lose track of it	to fail to understand any more
to lose time	(a clock or watch) to run slow

Train Yourself

Fill the gaps in the following sentences with expressions using the verb »lose«:

1. One year after I __________ my wife in a road accident I __________ to her sister.
2. He's not a very good speaker. After ten minutes I __________ of what he was trying to say.
3. She really should persist with that job and not __________ so quickly.

4. I know it's very irritating, but he doesn't have to __________ like that.
5. I'll have to take this watch back, it's __________.
6. The company couldn't keep pace with the competition and rapidly __________.

Talk Talk Talk

J. David here is a good man to know, Peter. I should have introduced you to him long ago. He **kept Ergo afloat** when we first started out. It wasn't easy, but David had faith in us.

J. Es ist gut, einen Mann wie David zu kennen, Peter. Ich hätte Sie ihm schon längst vorstellen sollen. Er **hielt Ergo über Wasser**, als wir anfingen. Es war nicht leicht, aber David hatte Vertrauen in uns.

D. It's part of a **bank manager**'s job to recognize **investment potential**. I recognized at the start that Ergo's **business plan** was a sound one. It's not difficult then to find the necessary **financial backing**.

D. Es ist Teil des Jobs eines **Bankmanagers**, **Investitionspotenzial** zu erkennen. Ich erkannte von Anfang an, dass der **Geschäftsplan** von Ergo vernünftig war. Dann ist es nicht schwer, die nötige **finanzielle Unterstützung** zu finden.

P. Well, I shall certainly be glad to follow your advice if ever I have to seek it.

P. Nun, ich werde sicher gerne Ihrem Rat folgen, wenn ich ihn einmal brauchen sollte.

J. And that might be more often than you imagine, Peter.

J. Und das könnte öfter sein als Sie sich vorstellen, Peter.

(adressing David) Peter here has to **take on** more and more **responsibilities** as **the company grows**. His New York trip was part of that. Now he has to return to Glasgow to **manage the operation** there.

(zu David) Peter muss mehr und mehr **Verantwortung übernehmen**, da die **Firma wächst**. Seine Reise nach New York war ein Teil davon. Jetzt muss er nach Glasgow zurückkehren, um **die Geschäfte** dort zu **führen**.

D. Then you must let me recommend to you our Scottish **office**. Ian McGregor manages our affairs there, although his office is in Edinburgh, not Glasgow.

D. Dann lassen Sie mich Ihnen unser schottisches **Büro** empfehlen. Ian McGregor führt dort unsere Geschäfte, obwohl sich sein Büro in Edinburgh und nicht in Glasgow befindet.

P. I always welcome a chance to get to Edinburgh. I'd certainly like to **make contact with** Mr McGregor.

P. Mir ist jede Möglichkeit recht, um nach Edinburgh zu kommen. Ich werde selbstverständlich gerne **Kontakt mit** Mr McGregor **aufnehmen**.

D. **Here's his card.** I'll call him to expect you to call.

D. **Hier ist seine Karte.** Ich werde ihn anrufen, um ihm zu sagen, dass er Ihren Anruf erwarten darf.

Train Yourself

This or that?
Complete the following sentences with the correct form:

1. You want to know what our response will be if a takeover bid is made? ____________ depends.
2. I don't like the look of these accounts at all. I'll have to look into ____________.
3. Will I get angry if they refuse our offer? ____________ is a good question.
4. Sit down, and let me explain how best to tackle the problem. I recommend going about it ____________ way.
5. ____________ is not the way to behave in these circumstances.
6. ____________ one, over there? I much prefer ____________ one here.

Vocabulary

to allow	erlauben
assistant	Assistent, Stellvertreter
at business	im Geschäft
to attend (a conference)	teilnehmen (an einer Konferenz)
bank manager	Bankmanager
to be bound	sicher sein
to be one's area of business	das Geschäftsgebiet von jemandem sein
to be on secondment	abgeordnet sein
business plan	Geschäftsplan
busy	beschäftigt
to catch up	aufholen
to chase	hinter etwas her sein, etwas verfolgen
commission charge	Provision
conference	Konferenz
conferencing	das Konferieren
to discuss the conference	die Konferenz besprechen
electronic communication	elektronische Kommunikation
electronics symposium	Elektronik-Symposium
everything in one's power	alles in seiner Macht Stehende
expansion	Expansion, Ausbreitung
experienced	erfahren, routiniert
financial backing	finanzielle Unterstützung
to get along	zurechtkommen, weiterkommen
to get down to work	sich an die Arbeit machen
to grow (e.g. a company)	wachsen (z. B. eine Firma)
Here's his/her card.	Hier ist seine/ihre (Visiten-) Karte.
high-tech	Hightech
I'm sorry to disturb you.	Es tut mir Leid, Sie zu stören.
I'm very pleased to meet you.	Ich freue mich, Ihre Bekanntschaft zu machen.
import-export business	Import-Export-Unternehmen
in business	beruflich

in good hands	in guten Händen
investment potential	Investitionspotenzial
to keep afloat	über Wasser halten
to keep up	mithalten
line	Branche
to make contact with	Kontakt aufnehmen mit
market	Markt
networking	Networking
office	Büro
operation	Unternehmen
to organize a meeting	eine Besprechung organisieren
to organize press conferences	Pressekonferenzen organisieren
promotion	Werbung
to put somebody in charge of	jemandem die Verantwortung übertragen für
routine	Routine
to run (a business)	(ein Unternehmen) leiten
sales staff	Verkaufspersonal
schedule	Terminkalender
software	Software
to specialize	spezialisieren
to start with a company	bei einer Firma anfangen
strong position	starke Position/Stellung
to take a message	eine Nachricht entgegennehmen
to take on responsibilities	Verantwortung übernehmen
to take over	übernehmen
team	Team, Mannschaft
The work's fine.	Die Arbeit läuft gut.
virtual conference	virtuelle Konferenz
What do you do, if I may ask?	Was machen Sie, wenn ich fragen darf?
when it comes to	etwas betreffen
to widen the circle of contacts	den Kontaktkreis erweitern

The conference
Die Konferenz

Here we go

Peter nimmt an einer Konferenz über Informationstechnologie teil, bei der er zahlreiche wichtige Kontakte knüpft und die Bekanntschaft eines Ministers macht, der die Veranstaltung eröffnet. Er geht mit dem Minister zum Mittagessen und macht offensichtlich Eindruck, da er bei seiner Rückkehr ins Büro einen Anruf aus dem Ministerium erhält ...

Talk Talk Talk

P. Hello, Beryl? Can you find the time this afternoon to come to my office and **fill me in** on this conference I shall be attending.	P. Hallo Beryl? Haben Sie heute Nachmittag Zeit, um in mein Büro zu kommen und mich über die Konferenz zu **informieren**, an der ich teilnehmen soll?
B. Certainly, Peter. I'll be there in ten minutes. Just let me **get done with** this piece of work on my desk. I'll send Chip around with **the relevant papers**, so you can start to read in ...	B. Selbstverständlich, Peter. Ich werde in zehn Minuten da sein. Lassen Sie mich nur das bisschen Arbeit auf meinem Tisch **erledigen**. Ich schicke Chip mit den **nötigen Papieren** vorbei, damit Sie anfangen können, sich einzulesen ...
P. Chip! Hello there! How are you? How's work going?	P. Chip! Hallo! Guten Tag! Wie geht's? Was macht die Arbeit?
C. Fine, thanks, Mr Brückner.	C. Danke gut, Mr Brückner.
P. So what have you got there for me?	P. Was haben Sie mir denn mitgebracht?

C. Ms Platt sent these papers round for you. She says take a butcher's at them and she'll be here in a jiffy. She's on her way up the apples and pears right now – I can hear her.

C. Ms Platt lässt Ihnen diese Papiere hier zukommen. Sie möchte, dass Sie einen Blick darauf werfen; sie wird in ein paar Minuten hier sein. Sie steigt gerade die Treppe herauf – ich kann sie hören.

P. Now, **come off it**, Chip. I know you're just having me on with all that cockney slang ...

P. Jetzt **hören** Sie **auf** damit, Chip. Ich weiß, Sie nehmen mich auf den Arm mit diesem ganzen Cockney-Slang ...

Background Information

We were introduced to some of Chip's rhyming **cockney** slang. Do you know the meaning of a butcher's? It's short for butcher's hook – which conveniently rhymes with »look«. So a butcher's is a »look« – »Are those your holiday snaps? Give me a butcher's!« Other very expressive cockney slang expressions include »Burton-on-Trent« for »rent«, »trouble-and-strife« for »wife« and several based on the use of »apples«: apples and pears (»stairs«), apple pie (»sky«) and apple-pips (»lips«).
It used to be said that a true cockney had to be born within the sound of the bells of Bow Church in the east end of London, but that's no longer the case. You'll now hear many Londoners from as far afield as the western suburbs calling themselves cockneys.

Train Yourself

Beryl tells Peter she has to *get done* with the work in front of her – meaning she has to finish it. **Replace the words and expressions using »done« in the following sentences with alternative expressions:**

1. The meal was delicious. The joint of beef was *done* to perfection.

....

2. I'm not very good at chess. Now you've taken my queen *I'm done for.*

3. The team was *done* after that exhausting game.

4. In polite company it's *not done* to eat peas off the blade of your knife, you know!

Talk Talk Talk

P. Come in, Beryl. I've only had a chance to **take a brief glance at** these papers – in fact, all I know at the moment is that this **conference is devoted** to advances in information technology and that it lasts four days. I'm glad **it's being held** here in London. I've done enough travelling for a while.

P. Kommen Sie herein, Beryl. Ich konnte bisher nur einen **kurzen Blick** auf die Papiere **werfen** – ich weiß im Augenblick lediglich, dass die **Konferenz** den Fortschritten der Informationstechnologie **gewidmet ist** und vier Tage dauert. Ich bin froh, **dass sie** hier in London **abgehalten wird**. Ich bin für eine Zeit lang genug gereist.

B. Yes, in fact that's why Mr Morgan has **registered** Ergo to attend. He doesn't want you back in Glasgow until the New Year, so the conference **fits nicely** into your schedule.

B. Ja, genau deshalb hat Mr Morgan Ergo zur Teilnahme **angemeldet**. Er möchte nicht, dass Sie vor Neujahr nach Glasgow zurückgehen, deshalb **passt** die Konferenz **gut** in Ihren Terminkalender.

P. Let's have a look at the programme. There are some interesting **speakers**, I see – including some from abroad.

P. Gehen wir das Programm durch. Wie ich sehe, gibt es einige interessante **Referenten** – inklusive einiger aus dem Ausland.

B. That's also what interests Mr

B. Das ist es auch, was Mr

Morgan. Apparently, about sixty percent of the participants will be from abroad. It will be a very **international forum**. Mr Morgan believes it will be an ideal opportunity for us to **expand our network of contacts** and at the same time tap into new ideas and advances. He'll be attending some sessions himself, but he wants you to **see it through** from beginning to end.

Morgan interessiert. Offensichtlich werden ungefähr sechzig Prozent aus dem Ausland kommen. Es wird ein wirklich **internationales Forum** sein. Mr Morgan glaubt, es wird eine ideale Gelegenheit für uns sein, **unser Netz von Kontakten** zu **erweitern** und zur gleichen Zeit auf neue Ideen und Fortschritte zu stoßen. An einigen Veranstaltungen wird er selbst teilnehmen, aber er möchte, dass Sie von Anfang bis Ende **dabei sind**.

P. I'll be glad to, of course. I see a minister is **opening the conference** and that the first **session** will be addressed by Professor Karl Schlüter, of York University. He was one of my teachers in Hamburg – a very clever man and an excellent speaker …

P. Das mache ich natürlich gerne. Ich sehe, dass ein Minister **die Konferenz eröffnet** und die **Sitzung** von Professor Karl Schlüter von der Universität York geleitet wird. Er war in Hamburg einer meiner Lehrer – ein sehr kluger Mann und ein exzellenter Redner …

False Friends

The word **»devoted«** has subtle shades of meaning which often present difficulties for non-native English speakers. Peter has mastered one meaning with no problem – noting that the conference he is to attend will be »devoted« to the subject of information technology. The conference will **concern itself** entirely **with** this subject, the four days will be **dedicated** to the topic. The word also has a very religious sense, describing the act of dedicating oneself to a sacred cause or God – »She became a nun and devoted herself to God.« But it also has a more mundane meaning, describing in sometimes exaggerated form an intense liking or love – »He's devoted to his family«, »I'm devoted to oysters«.

Background Information

Beryl tells Peter the conference **»fits nicely«** into his schedule, meaning there's room for it in Peter's working week. This is the most common form of **»fit«** – others include:

a good fit	well-tailored, (in carpentry) well made
to fit in (with)	to be in harmony or accord (with), to accommodate oneself
fit/fitting	suitable, appropriate
fits and starts	in an erratic manner
fit to be tied	extremely irritated or angry
fit to burst	replete, full of food; helpless with laughter
fit to kill	in an extravagant or striking manner

Train Yourself

Find the correct form of »fit« to fit the gaps in the following sentences:

1. I think there's something wrong with the car – it goes by ________.
2. No more for me thanks. It was delicious, but I'm ________.
3. I don't really mind what we do. I'll just ________ with the rest.
4. Where are you off to tonight? You look ________.
5. I'm so damned angry I'm ________.
6. You look very smart in that new outfit, it's a very ________.
7. I find it very ________ that Susan should be taking over the company founded by her father.
8. Do your plans ________ with ours?

Talk Talk Talk

(Ergo offices; four days later)

(Ergo-Büros; vier Tage später)

B. Now, do you have everything,

B. Haben Sie jetzt alles, Peter?

Peter? You know where the **conference venue** is?

Sie wissen, wo der **Konferenzort** ist?

P. I certainly hope so, Beryl. I'd be in trouble if I didn't, wouldn't I?

P. Das hoffe ich doch, Beryl. Ich wäre in Schwierigkeiten, wenn ich das nicht täte, stimmt's?

B. After your Glasgow mix-up nothing would surprise me.

B. Nach Ihrem Durcheinander in Glasgow würde mich nichts überraschen.

P. But Steve's not organizing this, thank goodness.

P. Aber Gott sei Dank wird das Ganze diesmal nicht von Steve organisiert.

B. That's another reason why you're going, and not Steve. Mr Morgan wants nothing to go wrong.

B. Das ist ein weiterer Grund, warum Sie gehen und nicht Steve. Mr Morgan will nicht, dass etwas schief geht.

P. That sounds a bit intimidating, Beryl.

P. Beryl, das klingt ein bisschen einschüchternd.

B. Don't worry, we're all expecting you to **come through with flying colours**. Now, here's your accreditation and your pass, two copies of the conference **programme**, an **advance copy** of the minister's speech. The invitations to the Ergo cocktail party are still being printed, but I'll send Chip around with them this afternoon. So, off you go. All the best – toi, toi, toi, as you say. I love that expression. You see, Peter, we're learning from you, too.

B. Keine Bange, wir erwarten alle, dass Sie **mit fliegenden Fahnen durchkommen**. Nun, hier ist Ihre Akkreditierung und Ihr Pass, zwei Kopien des Konferenz**programms**, eine **Vorabkopie** der Rede des Ministers. Die Einladungen für die Ergo-Cocktailparty werden noch gedruckt, aber ich schicke Chip heute Nachmittag damit vorbei. So, los geht's. Alles Gute – toi, toi, toi, wie Sie sagen. Ich liebe diesen Ausdruck. Sie sehen, Peter, wir lernen auch von Ihnen.

P. Thanks, Beryl. Just remind me once again of the best way of getting there. I don't want to take a taxi in this traffic.

P. Danke, Beryl. Sagen Sie mir doch noch einmal, wie ich am besten dort hinkomme. Ich möchte bei diesem Verkehr kein Taxi nehmen.

B. Take the Central line to Oxford Circus, and then it's two stops on the Piccadilly line. The hotel is right opposite the tube station ... Oh, Peter! Haven't you forgotten something?

B. Nehmen Sie die Central Line zum Oxford Circus und dann zwei Haltestellen mit der Piccadilly-Linie. Das Hotel ist genau gegenüber der U-Bahn-Station ... Oh, Peter! Haben Sie nicht etwas vergessen?

P. Beryl?

P. Beryl?

B. Your umbrella – it's raining cats and dogs outside ...

B. Ihren Regenschirm – draußen regnet es in Strömen ...

Train Yourself

Some revision ...

Peter says he would be in trouble if he didn't know the venue of the conference he is to attend – using the verb form *would* in an auxiliary function to express probability. *Would* has many such uses – **complete the following sentences with the correct forms to use with »would«:**

1. I would have won that contract if the company __________ (*submit*) the tender in time.
2. We would have come if we __________ (*receive*) the invitation.
3. Dave would be in very big trouble if the boss __________ (*know*) about his mistake.
4. His explanation would appear __________ (*be*) satisfactory.
5. The team would have won if it __________ (*try*) harder from the start of the game.
6. I wouldn't worry if I __________ (*be*) you.

Talk Talk Talk

(Lansdown Hotel; central London)

(Lansdown Hotel; Zentrum Londons)

P. Good morning! I'm here for the **conference on information technology**. Is this the **information desk**?

P. Guten Morgen! Ich bin wegen der **Informationstechnologie-Konferenz** hier. Ist das der **Informationsschalter?**

Receptionist: Yes, it is. **Are you accredited?**

Empfangsdame: Ja, das ist er. **Sind Sie akkreditiert?**

P. Yes, my name is Brückner. Peter Brückner, from Ergo Limited.

P. Ja, mein Name ist Brückner. Peter Brückner, von Ergo Limited.

R. Let me see. Yes, here's your name on the list. Let me give you this **information pack**, these meal vouchers and two **name-tags**. The conference **is taking place** in the Regency Room. Coffee and afternoon tea are served in the foyer, and lunch is in the main dining room. The Regency Room is that way.

R. Lassen Sie mich nachsehen. Ja, Ihr Name steht hier auf der Liste. Nehmen Sie bitte dieses **Infopaket**, diese Essensgutscheine und zwei **Namensschilder**. Die Konferenz **findet** im Regency Room **statt**. Kaffee und Nachmittagstee werden im Foyer serviert und Mittagessen gibt es im großen Speisesaal. Zum Regency Room geht es da entlang.

P. Thank you. I'm a little early. Is the room already open?

P. Danke. Ich bin ein bisschen früh dran. Ist der Raum bereits geöffnet?

R. Yes, you can go in now and take any place that pleases you.

R. Ja, Sie können jetzt hineingehen und Platz nehmen, wo Sie möchten.

(Regency Room)
P. Ah, you're also an **early customer**, I see. Is this place taken?

(Regency Room)
P. Ah, ich sehe, Sie sind auch ein **Überpünktlicher**. Ist dieser Platz besetzt?

Roy Noble: No, I'd be glad if you took it. I'm feeling a bit isolated in this vast room. I thought the conference started at nine thirty, so I'm **a good half hour early**.

Roy Noble: Nein, es würde mich freuen, wenn Sie Platz nehmen würden. Ich fühle mich etwas verloren in diesem riesigen Raum. Ich dachte, die Konferenz würde um neun Uhr dreißig beginnen, also bin ich eine **gute halbe Stunde zu früh dran**.

P. I was surprised how quickly I got here. The London transport system isn't as bad as many people **make out**.

P. Ich war erstaunt, wie schnell ich hierher gekommen bin. Das Londoner Verkehrssystem ist nicht so schlecht, wie manche Leute **behaupten**.

R. You're not from London?

R. Sie kommen nicht aus London?

P. No, I work for a **London-based company**, but I'm German. Peter Brückner, of Ergo Limited.

P. Nein, ich arbeite für eine **Firma mit Sitz in London**, aber ich bin Deutscher. Peter Brückner von Ergo Limited.

R. Ergo? I've heard of the company. My name is Roy Noble, of Noble Electronics. We **deal** mostly **in semiconductors** ... Business isn't too good at the moment because of the **slump** in the **new technology area**. How are you **faring**?

R. Ergo? Ich habe von dieser Firma gehört. Mein Name ist Roy Noble, von Noble Electronics. Wir **handeln** hauptsächlich **mit Halbleitern** ... Das Geschäft läuft im Moment nicht allzu gut wegen der **Wirtschaftskrise** auf dem **Gebiet der Neuen Technologien**. Wie **geht** es bei Ihnen?

P. Actually, not bad at all. We're even on an **expansion course**.

P. Gar nicht schlecht zurzeit. Wir sind sogar auf **Expansionskurs**.

R. How do you manage that?

R. Wie schaffen Sie das?

P. I think one reason is **diversification**. We have spread our activities

P. Ich glaube, ein Grund lautet **Diversifikation.** Wir haben unsere over a wide area. When one **sector weakens** we can **switch attention** to a stronger or **more promising** one.

Aktivitäten auf ein weites Gebiet ausgebreitet. Wenn ein **Sektor schwächer wird**, können wir unsere **Aufmerksamkeit** auf einen stärkeren oder **vielversprechenderen** verlagern.

R. I'd like to hear more – but it looks as if we're about to get under way ...

R. Ich würde gerne mehr erfahren – aber es sieht so aus, als würden wir gleich loslegen ...

Background Information

Don't be shy ...

Legendary English reserve is cast aside in **networking** and **business dealings**. Peter has an empty room in which to find a seat, but wisely chooses to place himself next to another early arrival and to **engage him** immediately **in conversation**. Since they are attending the same conference they obviously have much in common. Each has nothing to lose, and everything to gain, by overcoming any natural reserve and making direct contact.

Train Yourself

Multiple choice

1. We'll have to stay here for the night, I don't think the storm is going to let ________ (*with, down, up, against*).
2. That mail order company really let us ________ (*up, down, in, over*) – they promised delivery within three days but we're still waiting for the parcel.
3. If that's John at the door, can you let him ________ (*up, down, in, out*)?
4. We're giving Sue a surprise party on her fortieth birthday – please don't let ________ (*up, in, on, down*).
5. Can't we let Mike ________ (*in, on, in on, up on*) the secret?

6. The police could find no evidence against the arrested man so they let him ________ (*on, go, run, up*).
7. Judy let ________ (*on, up, out, in*) a big cry of recognition when they stepped off the train.
8. Don't let ________ (*over, on, up, in*) now. We don't have much further to go.

Talk Talk Talk

R. Well, I found the minister's speech very interesting, he obviously has **a good grasp of** the subject. It always surprises me how quickly ministers **get to grips with** the speciality they have been assigned ... Well, perhaps there is a future for us as Ministers of Information Technology or some such department! Another coffee? The break lasts half an hour ...

R. Nun, ich fand die Rede des Ministers sehr interessant, er hat das Thema offensichtlich **gut im Griff**. Es erstaunt mich immer, wie schnell sich Minister **mit** den speziellen Themen **auseinandersetzen**, die ihnen übertragen wurden ... Nun, vielleicht gibt es für uns eine Zukunft als Minister für Informationstechnologie oder in einem ähnlichen Ministerium! Noch einen Kaffee? Die Pause dauert eine halbe Stunde ...

Session chairman: Roy! I'd like you to meet the minister. Minister, Roy Noble here is an example of the **new entrepreneurship** abroad in Europe.

Konferenzleiter: Roy! Ich möchte Ihnen den Herrn Minister vorstellen. Herr Minister, Roy Noble hier ist ein Beispiel **neuen Unternehmertums** drüben in Europa.

R. How do you do, sir? Mr Brückner and I were just talking about your most interesting **address** to the conference.

R. Guten Tag, Sir. Herr Brückner und ich haben uns gerade über Ihre höchst interessante **Ansprache** an die Konferenz unterhalten.

Minister: Herr Brückner? Sie sind Deutscher? Es freut mich sehr Sie

Minister: Herr Brückner? Sie sind Deutscher? Es freut mich sehr, Sie kennen zu lernen – but, please, spare me the **embarrassment** of having to delve deeper into my inadequate **knowledge** of your language, and tell me what brings a German such as yourself to London and to a conference such as this.

kennen zu lernen – aber bitte, ersparen Sie mir die **Peinlichkeit**, tiefer in meinen unzulänglichen **Kenntnissen** Ihrer Sprache zu graben und erzählen Sie mir, was einen Deutschen wie Sie nach London und zu einer Konferenz wie dieser hier führt.

P. I'm afraid the coffee break isn't long enough, minister. It's a long story.

P. Ich fürchte, die Kaffeepause ist nicht lang genug, Herr Minister. Das ist eine lange Geschichte.

Minister: Then do **join** my party for lunch. We're table number one, isn't that so, Leo?

Minister: Dann **schließen** Sie sich zu Mittag meiner Gesellschaft an. Wir haben Tisch Nummer eins, nicht wahr, Leo?

False Friends

Be careful in distinguishing between the verbs **»assign«** and **»resign«**. Assign is a transitive verb with the chief meaning of **giving responsibility** to somebody – »I assigned her the job of maintaining contact with branch offices«. Resign is used mainly in an intransitive sense, where it means to **relinquish** – »After losing the vote of confidence the prime minister resigned«.

Talk Talk Talk

(Lansdown Hotel's dining room)

(Lansdown Hotel, Speisesaal)

R. Where's table number one? Ah, there!

R. Wo ist Tisch Nummer eins? Ah, dort!

P. **May we join you**, as you kindly suggested, minister?

P. **Dürfen wir uns zu Ihnen setzen**, wie Sie so freundlich vorschlugen, Herr Minister?

M. Certainly, certainly. Do sit down. And how did you find the professor's **contribution**?

M. Sicher, sicher. Nehmen Sie Platz. Und wie fanden Sie den **Beitrag** des Professors?

P. Very interesting indeed.

P. Wirklich sehr interessant.

R. Same here. And some very interesting points were **raised** in the discussion afterwards.

R. Das meine ich auch. Und es wurden einige interessante Punkte in der Diskussion danach **aufgebracht**.

M. I thought so, too. It's encouraging to hear so many new ideas and new interpretations of what we – I speak for myself, of course – often take for granted. The new technologies are forcing us to appraise old approaches. We just have to break out of **timeworn** practices and join the drive forwards or get left behind. This really is a revolution. Is this the way you see things in Germany, Mr Brückner?

M. Das fand ich auch. Es ist ermutigend, so viele neue Ideen und neue Interpretationen davon zu hören, was wir – ich spreche natürlich für mich selbst – oft als gegeben hinnehmen. Die Neuen Technologien zwingen uns, alte Errungenschaften abzuschätzen. Wir müssen einfach aus **ausgedienten** Praktiken ausbrechen und uns dem Vorstoß anschließen oder wir werden hinterherhinken. Das ist wirklich eine Revolution. Sehen Sie in Deutschland die Dinge auch auf diese Weise, Mr Brückner?

P. I think so, minister. I can really speak only for my own company.

P. Ich denke schon, Herr Minister. Ich kann wirklich nur für meine eigene Firma sprechen.

M. And that is?

M. Und das ist?

P. Ergo Limited.

P. Ergo Limited.

M. Very **far-sighted**, I'm sure. Very impressive. Tell me more about this Ergo ...

M. Sicherlich sehr **weitsichtig**. Sehr beeindruckend. Erzählen Sie mir mehr von dieser Ergo ...

Background Information

The government minister tells Peter many new technological advances are **taken for granted** – meaning they are accepted without much further thought or appreciation. We have already met several expressions using **»take«** – and now here are some more:

to take account of	to include in an assessment
to take a dim (or poor) view of something	to disapprove
to take charge	to assume control or custody
to take heart	to gain courage or confidence
to take hold	to grasp, to seize
to take in vain	to use somebody or somebody's name without respect
to take note	to commit to memory
to take stock	to make an assessment or valuation
to take the cake	to win, to claim first place
to take to task	to criticize, to call to account

Train Yourself

Complete the following sentences using expressions with »take«:

1. The company made record profits last year. That ________.
2. ________ this advice. You'll find it very useful in the future.
3. Let's sit down and with cool heads ________ the situation.
4. The staff has ________ from the good news coming from head office.
5. The board was very dissatisfied with the performance of its chairman, and severely ________.
6. The shop-floor manager ________ workers arriving late and leaving early.
7. Did you ________ the stock market plunge in working out those figures?
8. Are we all here? So who's going to ________ the meeting?

Talk Talk Talk

M. Well, it's time for the **second session** to start, and it's time for me to be off. I'd like to stay, but there's work at the Ministry.

M. Nun, es ist Zeit für die **zweite Sitzung** und es ist Zeit für mich, zu gehen. Ich würde gerne bleiben, aber ich habe im Ministerium zu tun.

P. **I'm very happy to have met you**, and thank you very much for your patience in listening to my **description** of what we do and what we plan.

P. **Es war mir eine große Freude, Sie kennen zu lernen** und ich danke Ihnen sehr herzlich für Ihre Geduld, mit der Sie meiner **Beschreibung**, was wir tun und was wir vorhaben, zugehört haben.

M. Not at all, Mr Brückner. You didn't do all the talking, by any means. Mr Noble here had a lot to say about his **enterprise**. I have learnt a lot from you both, and I wish you all the very best in your extremely **worthwhile endeavours**.

M. Ich bitte Sie, Mr Brückner. Sie haben gar nicht die ganze Zeit über geredet. Mr Noble hier hatte viel über sein **Unternehmen** zu erzählen. Ich habe viel von Ihnen beiden gelernt und ich wünsche Ihnen das Allerbeste bezüglich Ihres ausgesprochen **lohnenden Bestrebens**.

R. Thank you very much, minister.

R. Vielen Dank, Herr Minister.

P. Yes, thank you very much indeed.

P. Ja, ich danke Ihnen wirklich vielmals.

M. Well then, goodbye. I must be on my way ...

M. Also dann, auf Wiedersehen. Ich muss mich auf den Weg machen.

J. Hello Peter! Ready for the second session then? I missed **the opening of the conference** and the

J. Hallo Peter! Sind Sie denn bereit für die zweite Sitzung? Ich habe die **Eröffnung der Konferenz** und

lunch. There's so much to do back at the office. But I did want to catch the address by the **head** of the British Electronics Association. There's **bound to be** some interesting discussion afterwards.

das Mittagessen versäumt. Im Büro ist so viel zu tun. Aber ich wollte den Vortrag des **Vorsitzenden** der British Electronics Association nicht verpassen. Danach gibt es **bestimmt** eine interessante Diskussion.

P. Should I return to the office, do you think?

P. Glauben Sie, ich sollte zum Büro zurückkehren?

J. No, not at all. It's **in good hands** – Beryl and that clever young nephew of hers **are in charge**. And Steve is **looking by** later today.

J. Nein, gar nicht. Es ist **in guten Händen** – Beryl und ihr kluger junger Neffe **kümmern sich darum**. Und Steve **schaut** heute noch **vorbei**.

P. Steve? I thought he was in Glasgow.

P. Steve? Ich dachte, er wäre in Glasgow.

J. He's **fairly well wrapped things up** there. He **got moving** for a change – I suspect he couldn't wait to get back to London.

J. Er hat die **Sachen** dort **ziemlich gut abgewickelt**. Er **hat sich** diesmal **beeilt** – ich vermute, er konnte es nicht abwarten, nach London zurückzukehren.

Background Information

From the exchange between the minister and Peter Brückner it is clear that Peter has not **hogged the conversation**. He also **drew his other table companion**, Roy Noble, **into the discussion** – a wise and diplomatic move, particularly in dealing with politicians!

Train Yourself

Watch those tenses!

The minister tells Peter and Roy Noble he is very happy to have met them – indicating by his use of the past tense the meeting is now over.

Select the correct tenses to use in the following sentences:

1. I was disappointed to __________ (*miss*) her when she called.
2. I am very happy to __________ (*hear*) that you __________ (*recover*) from that very serious operation.
3. They said they were very relieved to __________ (*catch*) us before we __________ (board) the plane.
4. I was angry for days after __________ (*hear)* that he __________ (*leave*) that job of work unfinished.
5 I hoped to __________ (*meet*) you, but it __________ (*be*) not to be.
6. I am very glad to __________ (*find*) you at home and to say how sorry I __________ (*be*) for all that has happened.

Talk Talk Talk

J. I can use this coffee break. All those **facts and figures** are **scrambling my brain**.	J. Ich kann diese Kaffeepause brauchen. All diese **Fakten und Zahlen schwirren** mir noch **im Kopf herum**.
P. I **recorded** it all, if you'd like to **go over** it later.	P. Ich habe alles **aufgenommen**, falls Sie es später **durchgehen** wollen.
J. Recorded it? How?	J. Es aufgenommen? Wie?
P. This **pocket recorder** here. It's very handy. It **picks up** everything.	P. Dieser **Taschenrekorder** hier. Er ist sehr handlich. Er **nimmt** alles **auf**.
J. Well, I'll be damned! I didn't think of that. Well done!	J. Donnerwetter! Daran habe ich nicht gedacht. Gut gemacht!
P. Will you be staying for the **final session**?	P. Werden Sie bis zur **Abschlusssitzung** bleiben?
J. No, I have to get moving. But, look, do join me for a drink afterwards. You can then fill me in on	J. Nein, ich muss weg. Aber gehen wir danach doch noch auf einen Drink. Sie können mich dann über

the rest of the **day's proceedings**. I'll wait for you at the office. That is, if you **have** nothing else **in mind**.

den Rest des **Tagesverlaufs** informieren. Ich werde im Büro auf Sie warten. Das heißt, wenn Sie nichts anderes **vorhaben**.

P. No, I've **kept my appointments book clear** for the duration of the conference. I'll come straight back to the office after the session ends.

P. Nein, **ich habe** mir für die Dauer der Konferenz **meinen Terminkalender freigehalten**. Ich komme nach Ende der Sitzung direkt ins Büro.

J. And bring that tape with you, if you would. Very useful. Well done, Peter!

J. Und würden Sie das Band mitbringen? Sehr nützlich. Gut gemacht, Peter!

Background Information

The clever businessperson always has a small **tape-recorder** at the ready. It's as useful as a **pocket diary** or **calculator**. But be sure to draw attention to it in any business encounter and to request permission to use it.

At the ready? That means ready for immediate use. **At hand** – an expression we've already encountered – has the same meaning.

A tape-recorder picks up sounds. There are several other useful expressions using »pick«:

to pick and choose	to select with care
to pick at	to nag, to criticize repeatedly
to pick on	to single out for criticism or special attention
to pick (one's way)	to proceed slowly and carefully
to pick out	to discern, to make out
to pick up	to buy or acquire casually or by chance; to learn something; to catch a disease or a cold; to catch sight of; to resume or continue; to improve; to increase in speed or strength

to pick up on	to notice, to become aware of something

Train Yourself

Fill the gaps in the following sentences with expressions employing »pick«:

1. Why ________ her? The whole department was to blame, if you ask me.
2. Did you ________ the signals his speech was sending out? Their message was unmistakable.
3. Can you ________ the outline of the mountains, over there on the horizon?
4. The nice thing about this new shop is that you can ________ at leisure.
5. How do you like this picture I ________ in the antique shop in High Street?
6. They ________ along the rough path as if it were a minefield.
7. Did you ________ his change of tone, the way he now emphasizes the problems we are facing?
8. The car rapidly ________ speed as the road became wider.
9. I can't face dinner at the Thompsons. His wife is constantly ________ poor John.
10. He seems to have ________ a nasty virus on that trip to India.

Talk Talk Talk

(Ergo offices)	(Ergo-Büros)
L. Peter? I have a call for you from the **Ministry of Overseas Trade**.	L. Peter? Ich habe ein Gespräch für Sie vom **Außenhandelsministerium**.
P. The Ministry of Overseas Trade? Are you sure, Lucy?	P. Das Außenhandelsministerium? Sind Sie sicher, Lucy?

L. They **asked to speak to** Mr Brückner. I have a Mr Carter on the line. Shall I **put** him **through**?	L. Sie **wollten mit** Mr Brückner **sprechen**. Ich habe einen Mr Carter in der Leitung. Soll ich ihn **durchstellen**?
P. Yes, of course, Lucy. Hello? Peter Brückner here.	P. Ja natürlich, Lucy. Hallo? Hier ist Peter Brückner.
C. Mr Brückner. The minister has asked me to call you and ask if you would be kind enough to find the time to **attend a meeting** at the ministry next Tuesday. He is **meeting with a delegation** from the World Trade Organization and would value your presence.	C. Mr Brückner. Der Minister hat mich gebeten, Sie anzurufen und zu fragen, ob Sie so nett wären, sich nächsten Dienstag die Zeit zu nehmen, um **an einer Besprechung** im Ministerium **teilzunehmen**. Er **trifft sich** mit einer **Delegation** der Welthandelsorganisation und hätte Sie gerne dabei.
P. Me? What can I contribute?	P. Ich? Was kann ich beisteuern?
C. The minister only asked if you would agree to attend. He didn't tell me what role he envisaged for you. But he did suggest that if you could find the time you and I should get together before next Tuesday to **look at the agenda**. Would Friday be all right?	C. Der Minister fragte nur, ob Sie einverstanden wären, teilzunehmen. Er sagte mir nicht, welche Rolle er Ihnen zugedacht hat. Aber er hat vorgeschlagen, dass, falls Sie Zeit hätten, wir beide uns vor nächsten Dienstag treffen sollten, um **die Tagesordnung durchzugehen**. Würde Ihnen Freitag passen?
P. Just let me look in **my engagement book**. Ah, the conference is over on Thursday. Yes, Friday would be fine. When and where?	P. Lassen Sie mich kurz in **meinem Terminkalender** nachsehen. Ah, die Konferenz ist am Donnerstag vorbei. Ja, Freitag wäre schön. Wann und wo?
C. Here at the ministry, at eleven? Just ask for me at reception and	C. Hier im Ministerium, um elf Uhr? Fragen Sie einfach an der

they'll arrange to show you up.

Rezeption nach mir und man wird Ihnen den Weg zeigen.

P. I'll be there. Goodbye. Ah, James – you've just missed a most interesting conversation. The Ministry of Overseas Trade wants me to **participate in a meeting** there next week. I accepted, of course – I hope that's all right.

P. Ich werde da sein. Auf Wiederhören. Ah, James – Sie haben ein äußerst interessantes Gespräch verpasst. Das Außenhandelsministerium möchte, dass ich dort nächste Woche **an einer Besprechung teilnehme**. Ich habe natürlich zugesagt – ich hoffe, das ist in Ordnung.

J. Well, I hope we're not going to lose you to the government now. But, no, **in all seriousness** – **go for it**! You obviously made quite an impression on the minister ...

J. Nun, ich hoffe, wir verlieren Sie jetzt nicht an die Regierung. Aber, nein, **ganz im Ernst** – **gehen Sie hin**! Sie haben offensichtlich einen sehr positiven Eindruck auf den Minister gemacht ...

False Friends

»Show up« has two very different meanings. If you cause embarrassment to somebody you show him or her up. But if you show somebody up to a room or an office you guide them there, you show them the way.

Background Information

Let's show you now some everyday expressions employing the word **»show«**:

show business (showbiz)	the entertainment industry (principally the theatre and films)
showcase	a favourable setting in which something is displayed
showdown	a decisive confrontation or contest

showing	performance, appearance, presentation
showman	a person with the ability of projecting or presenting himself (also herself) effectively
to show off	to display or exhibit proudly, to seek to attract attention by extravagant or foolish behaviour
to show one's hand	to disclose one's intentions
showpiece	an oustanding example of something put on display
to show somebody the door	to eject somebody, to tell somebody to leave, to get out
showstopper	something or somebody of outstanding interest or beauty
showy	ostentatious, pretentious, vulgar

Train Yourself

Some revision

Do you remember your telephone vocabulary? Lucy tells Peter she has somebody from the Ministry of Overseas Trade on the line – meaning, of course, that somebody has called the Ergo offices asking to speak to Peter and Lucy has told him to wait while she puts him through.

Complete this telephone exchange correctly:

Lucy: __________, Ergo here. Can I __________ you?
Caller: Thatcher of North End Electronics here. I'd like to __________ __________ to Mr Morgan please.
L. I'll see if he's __________ . Just __________ a moment, please. Mr Morgan? I __________ a Mr Thatcher of North End Electronics __________. Shall I __________ him __________?
M. No, Lucy. I'm very busy at the moment. He's __________ about sales, so __________ him __________ Steve.
L. Hello, Mr Thatcher? Mr Morgan is __________ on another __________ at the moment. He has asked me to __________ you __________ Mr Blackman. Sorry to keep you __________.

I'll ______ you right away. Oh dear! Mr Blackman's ______ ______ is ______. Would you like to ______? His line should be ______ very soon.

C. No. I have a ______ waiting for me on another ______. I'll ______ back.

M. Hello Lucy? Is Thatcher still ______? I've just remembered something I wanted to ______ with him. Can you ______ ______ him ______?

L. No, Mr Morgan. He ______. He says he'll ______ later.

M. Lucy, this is rather important. Do you think you could ______ his number for me?

L. Well, he said something about having a ______ on another ______. But I'll try to ______ him for you.

The alternatives: *call, on the line, dial, reach, line, wait, hang up, have, put through, discuss, hold, busy, engaged, hang on, hello, in, connect*

Vocabulary

address	Ansprache
advance copy	Vorabkopie
to ask to speak to somebody	mit jemandem sprechen wollen
to attend a meeting	an einer Besprechung teilnehmen
to be accredited	akkreditiert sein
to be in charge	zuständig sein für, sich kümmern um
to be on one's way	auf dem Weg sein, wegmüssen
bound to be	bestimmt/sicher sein
to come off it	mit etwas aufhören
to come through with flying colours	mit fliegenden Fahnen durchkommen/Erfolg haben
conference on information technology	Informationstechnologie-Konferenz
conference venue	Konferenzort
contribution	(Rede-)Beitrag
day's proceedings	Tagesverlauf
to deal in semiconductors	mit Halbleitern handeln
description	Beschreibung

diversification	Diversifikation/breiteres Angebot
early customer	»früher Kunde«/früh dran sein, ein »Überpünktlicher«
embarrassment	Peinlichkeit, Verlegenheit
engagement book	Terminkalender
enterprise	Unternehmen
to expand the network of contacts	das Netz von Kontakten erweitern
facts and figures	Fakten und Zahlen
fairly well	ziemlich gut
to fare	ergehen
to fill somebody in	jemanden informieren
final session	Abschlusssitzung
to fit nicely	gut passen
to get done with something	etwas erledigen
to get to grips with	sich mit (etwas) auseinandersetzen
Go for it!	Gehen Sie hin!/Machen Sie das!
to go over	durchgehen
to have a good grasp of something	etwas gut im Griff haben
to have in mind	vorhaben
head	Vorsitzende(r)
I'm very happy to have met you.	Es war mir eine große Freude, Sie kennen zu lernen!
in all seriousness	ganz im Ernst
in good hands	in guten Händen
information desk	Informationsschalter
information pack	Infopaket
international forum	internationales Forum
to join somebody	sich zu jemandem setzen
to keep one's appointment book clear	seinen Terminkalender freihalten
knowledge	Kenntnisse
London-based company	Firma mit Sitz in London
to look at the agenda	die Tagesordnung durchgehen
to look by	vorbeischauen
to make out	etwas hinstellen als, behaupten
to meet with a delegation	sich mit einer Delegation treffen
Ministry of Overseas Trade	Außenhandelsministerium

name-tag	Namensschild
new entrepreneurship	neues Unternehmertum
new technology area	Gebiet der Neuen Technologie
to open the conference	eine Konferenz eröffnen
opening of a conference	Konferenzeröffnung
to participate in a meeting	an einer Besprechung teilnehmen
to pick up	aufnehmen
pocket recorder	Taschenrekorder
programme	Programm
promising	viel versprechend
to put somebody through	jemanden durchstellen
to raise	etwas aufbringen (z. B. Diskussionspunkte)
to record	aufnehmen, aufzeichnen
to register	anmelden, registrieren
relevant papers	nötige Papiere
to scramble the brain	im Kopf herumschwirren
sector	Sektor, Gebiet, Branche
to see something through	bei etwas dabei sein
session	Sitzung
slump	Wirtschaftskrise
speaker	Referent, Redner
to switch attention	Aufmerksamkeit verlagern
to take a brief glance at	einen kurzen Blick werfen auf
to take place	stattfinden
timeworn	ausgedient
to weaken	schwächen
to work for	für (etwas) arbeiten
worthwhile endeavours	lohnendes Bestreben/ Bemühungen
to wrap things up	Sachen abwickeln

International relations
Internationale Beziehungen

Here we go

Peter hat eine interessante Besprechung im Außenhandelsministerium und nimmt dann an einer Ministerkonferenz teil, wobei er den Minister erneut trifft und einige nützliche Anleitungen in internationalen Geschäftspraktiken sammelt. Er trifft auch wieder mit Archie Atherton-Smythe zusammen, der Peter zu einer Wochenendparty in seinem Haus auf dem Lande einlädt – wo Peter eine sehr angenehme Überraschung erwartet ...

Talk Talk Talk

(Ministry of Overseas Trade, London)

P. Good morning! I **have an appointment** with Mr Carter.

Receptionist: Just one moment. Let's see. Your name, please?

P. Brückner. Peter Brückner, of Ergo Limited.

R. Mr Brückner. Yes, here we are. Would you be so kind as to **sign the book** at this place. Here is a **visitor's pass**. Mr Carter's office is room 315 on the third floor. The lift is over there, on your right.

(Außenhandelsministerium, London)

P. Guten Morgen! Ich **habe eine Verabredung** mit Mr Carter.

Empfangsdame: Einen Moment bitte. Lassen Sie uns mal sehen. Ihr Name, bitte?

P. Brückner. Peter Brückner, von Ergo Limited.

E. Mr Brückner. Ja, hier steht es. Wären Sie so nett und würden hier **im Buch unterschreiben**. Hier ist ein **Besucherausweis**. Mr Carters Büro ist Zimmer 315 im dritten Stock. Der Lift ist dort hinten rechts.

P. Thank you ... Is this Mr Carter's office?

P. Danke ... Ist das Mr Carters Büro?

Secretary: Yes, it is. You must be Mr Brückner. Mr Carter is expecting you. Go right in please ...

Sekretärin: Ja, das ist es. Sie müssen Mr Brückner sein. Mr Carter erwartet Sie. Gehen Sie gleich hinein ...

P. Mr Carter? I'm Peter Brückner.

P. Mr Carter? Ich bin Peter Brückner.

C. Delighted to meet you. Please come in and sit down. Mollie, fetch Mr Brückner and me some coffee, please. Now, Mr Brückner, let me describe what the Minister **has in mind** for you. That is, if you would be so good as to agree to attend our conference next week ...

C. Freut mich, Sie kennen zu lernen. Bitte treten Sie ein und nehmen Sie Platz. Mollie, bringen Sie Mr Brückner und mir bitte Kaffee. Nun, Mr Brückner, lassen Sie mich beschreiben, was der Minister mit Ihnen **im Sinn hat**. Das heißt, wenn Sie so nett wären und an unserer Konferenz nächste Woche teilnehmen ...

Train Yourself

The secretary at the Ministry of Overseas Trade tells Peter he »must be« Mr Brückner – meaning she is sure he is that person. Uncertainty is expressed by »might«: »Might you be Mr Brückner, by any chance?«. **Select the correct form of must or might to use in the following sentences:**

1. That ______ be our bus coming now. It's the number 29, isn't it?
2. The company ______ surely be on the way to recovery by now. Its first quarter results were very good indeed.
3. You ______ be very tired after that long journey.
4. I ______ be interested in investing in your company if you can support your optimism with convincing evidence of potential improvement.
5. They ______ be interested in buying the house after Mr Jenning's convincing sales talk.

6. You ________ be the new sales manager, by all accounts.
7. Give me a week to think it over. I ________ be interested in taking on the job.
8. They're in such trouble they ________ be interested by now in selling the firm. I'm convinced of it.

Talk Talk Talk

C. At **multinational conferences** such as this one the Minister likes to find people from within the British business community who have **foreign experience** or **foreign experts** who are working here in Britain. You belong to the latter category.

C. Bei **multinationalen Konferenzen** wie dieser trifft der Minister gerne Leute aus der britischen Geschäftswelt, die über **Auslandserfahrung** verfügen oder **Auslandsexperten**, die hier in England arbeiten. Sie gehören zur letzteren Kategorie.

P. But my experience in the **international arena** is very limited.

P. Aber meine Erfahrung auf der **internationalen Bühne** ist sehr begrenzt.

C. That doesn't matter. You are a kind of bridge between the British business environment and Europe – I mean, of course, mainland Europe! In the same way, the Minister has invited business people with **practical knowledge** of **dealing in American, Asian and African markets**.

C. Das macht nichts. Sie bilden eine Art Brücke zwischen dem britischen Geschäftsumfeld und Europa – ich meine natürlich das europäische Festland! Der Minister hat ebenso Geschäftsleute mit **praktischen Handelserfahrungen auf amerikanischen, asiatischen und afrikanischen Märkten eingeladen**.

P. Are there differences?

P. Gibt es da Unterschiede?

C. Huge ones. I'm told you have just returned from a business trip to America. Didn't you notice any **differences in approach** between your contacts here and those you

C. Riesige. Ich hörte, Sie kommen gerade von einer Geschäftsreise von Amerika zurück. Sind Ihnen keine **Unterschiede in der Handlungsweise** zwischen Ihren Kontak-

made over there?

ten hier und denen, die Sie dort gemacht haben, aufgefallen?

P. Well, yes, I suppose I did. I found American business people even more informal than the British.

P. Nun ja, ich denke schon. Ich fand amerikanische Geschäftsleute sogar noch zwangloser als die britischen.

C. Exactly, although I think at our government level we are not that – what do the Americans say? – **laid back**!

C. Genau, obwohl ich glaube, dass wir in Regierungskreisen nicht so – wie sagen die Amerikaner? – **relaxed sind**!

Background Information

1. Many British people – even at an official level – still talk about Europe as if their country isn't part of the continent. The **»continent«** is exactly that: the land mass across the English Channel (»We're off to the continent on holiday tomorrow!«). The words »Europe« or »continent« to signify Europe without the British Isles are so ingrained in the English language that their use does not necessarily signal opposition to concepts of a united Europe. In the same way, the United States is »over there« – somewhere across the Atlantic Ocean!

2. Mr Carter uses an uncharacteristic slang expression here in describing the Americans – **laid-back**, meaning in this context »relaxed«. Lately, the expression has also come to mean »lazy« or »indifferent« – but Mr Carter is obviously not describing Americans in this way. There are several expressions employing **»laid«** or **»lay«**, including:

laid up	ill, disabled by injury
to lay (a bet)	to wager, to make a bet
layabout	a workshy person who lives off the State or off charity
to lay away (or lay in)	to put aside for future use, to store
to lay down	to surrender, to give up

to lay off	to discharge workers, usually temporarily
to lay on	to plan, to arrange, to organize
to lay on the table	to put an item on the agenda

Train Yourself

Complete the following sentences with the correct expression using »lay« or »laid«:

1. They __________ their arms at the approach of the opposing troops.
2. He caught a very nasty virus on his holiday in Africa and has been __________ for two months.
3. The government has drawn up new legislation, which will be __________ next week.
4. She is very worried about her son, who seems to have become a real __________.
5. The party was a great success, the Smiths __________ a magnificent feast.
6. Why don't you __________ some of your winnings for a rainy day?
7. I'll __________ ten to one that they won't succeed.
8. The company is doing so badly that it has had to __________ five hundred workers.

False Friends

Lay or lie?

The correct use of the verbs **»lay«** and **»lie«** has been debated for many years, and even the most eminent philologists can't agree among themselves. You're best advised to stay out of the argument and to remember just one basic rule: »lay« is normally a transitive verb (commanding an object) and »lie« an intransitive one (where no object is required). The difference is best seen in sentences such as: »Lay down your arms and lie on the floor!«

»I only wanted to lie down for ten minutes but I'd scarcely laid my head on the pillow than I slipped into a deep slumber.«
This exercise is good for the back: lie out straight on the floor, lay a heavy book on your feet and then raise your legs 20 times!

Talk Talk Talk

C. Ah, coffee! Thank you Mollie. How do you take yours, Mr Schröder?

C. Ah, Kaffee! Danke sehr, Mollie. Wie trinken Sie Ihren, Mr Schröder?

P. Brückner. The name's Brückner. Black, no sugar, please, Mr Carter.

P. Brückner. Mein Name ist Brückner. Schwarz, ohne Zucker bitte, Mr Carter.

C. Ah, dear me, I'm so sorry. I'm not so good with German names. Now, if you were Chinese I'd have no problem.

C. Ach du meine Güte, entschuldigen Sie. Ich tue mich schwer mit deutschen Namen. Nun, wenn Sie Chinese wären, hätte ich kein Problem.

P. You've **worked in China**?

P. Sie haben **in China gearbeitet**?

C. No, but I've had a lot of **dealings** with the Chinese, and I studied Mandarin at university.

C. Nein, aber ich habe viele **Verhandlungen** mit Chinesen geführt und ich habe an der Universität Mandarin studiert.

P. Then you must be quite the expert.

P. Dann müssen Sie ein ziemlicher Experte sein.

C. You know, you can study all you like in the classroom, but it's practical experience that counts. Take the Chinese. I came out of university quite fluent in Mandarin,

C. Wissen Sie, Sie können im Klassenzimmer studieren, was Sie wollen, aber es ist die praktische Erfahrung, die zählt. Nehmen Sie zum Beispiel die Chinesen. Ich

but I hadn't a clue how to speak effectively to Chinese visitors. And this applies to all Asian countries, you know.

habe die Universität mit ziemlich fließendem Mandarin verlassen, aber ich hatte keine Ahnung, wie ich wirklich mit den chinesischen Besuchern sprechen sollte. Und das gilt für alle asiatischen Länder, wissen Sie.

P. How do you mean exactly?

P. Wie meinen Sie das genau?

C. You must **approach a meeting** with Chinese people in a very specific way. Remember, the Chinese, and of course the Japanese – but also other Asian peoples – **hate to lose face**, so confrontation, impatience and particularly anger are to be avoided **at all costs**. This can be very frustrating for a Westerner, who might be misled by polite smiles and expressions of enthusiasm or agreement that a deal has been sealed. Not a bit! It takes great patience and knowledge of the Asian character to achieve success in that **difficult market**.

C. Sie müssen **an eine Verhandlung** mit Chinesen auf eine ganz bestimmte Art **herangehen**. Denken Sie daran, dass die Chinesen, und natürlich die Japaner – aber auch andere asiatische Völker – **es hassen, ihr Gesicht zu verlieren**, also müssen Konfrontationen, Ungeduld und besonders Ärger **um jeden Preis** vermieden werden. Das kann für einen Abendländer sehr frustrierend sein, der durch höfliches Lächeln und Ausdrücke der Begeisterung oder Zustimmung zu dem falschen Schluss kommen könnte, dass die Vereinbarung besiegelt worden ist. Kein bisschen! Es erfordert große Geduld und gute Kenntnisse des asiatischen Charakters, um auf diesem **schwierigen Markt** Erfolg zu erzielen.

P. How interesting. I have read similar assessments, but it's most interesting to hear this expressed at ministerial level.

P. Wie interessant. Ich habe über ähnliche Einschätzungen gelesen, aber es ist höchst interessant, das auf ministerialer Ebene ausgedrückt zu hören.

C. Don't mistake my comments for prejudice. Not a bit! In fact, I'm a great admirer of the **Asian business ethic**.

C. Verwechseln Sie meine Kommentare nicht mit Vorurteilen. Kein bisschen! Tatsächlich bin ich ein großer Bewunderer der **asiatischen Geschäftsethik**.

False Friends

Mr Carter tells Peter he's »so sorry« that he's **»not so good«** with German names. He's not using a comparative form here – »so« in this context means **»very«**. And if something is so-so it's neither good nor bad, it's average. Peter tells Mr Carter he must be **»quite the expert«** after studying Mandarin at university – here also, the word »quite« has acquired the meaning of »very« – »You must be very much an expert«. Note that when Mr Carter says he left university »quite« fluent in Mandarin he is being modest about his ability, which in fact is »quite« impressive. But be careful! »Quite« can have the meaning of »moderately« or »reasonably«, depending on the context and even on the inflexion in the way the word is pronounced. Peter tells Mr Carter that what he has had to say was **»most interesting«** – »most« here is not part of any comparative but also means »very«.

Train Yourself

Rewrite the following sentences to avoid using »quite« or »most«:

1. I didn't think the speaker was that good. His address to the forum, in fact was quite dull.

....

2. He thinks he's quite the expert, but he doesn't really know that much.

....

3. I'm most obliged to you for your assistance, which has been quite beyond the bonds of friendship.

....

4. She was quite the most beautiful bride I have ever seen.

5. I must say I'm quite interested in the job offer, although I can't quite make up my mind.

6. Her performance of that quite difficult task was most useful to us.

Talk Talk Talk

P. I am very interested in what you have to say because I believe Ergo is planning to **break into** the Asian market, difficult though that will be.

P. Ich habe großes Interesse an dem, was Sie zu sagen haben, da ich glaube, dass Ergo plant, **in** den asiatischen Markt **einzudringen**, so schwer das auch sein wird.

C. Oh, there are other tips I could give you then, if we had the time. I'll pass on just one more most important one: in any encounter with an Asian businessperson first **present your business card**. It's expected and appreciated. From then on in, you're on your own, as long as you remember to be polite and deferential at all times. Never, ever show impatience, irritation or anger. That will get you nowhere.

C. Oh, da könnte ich Ihnen noch weitere Tipps geben, wenn wir Zeit dazu hätten. Ich werde nur noch zu einem weiteren sehr wichtigen kommen: Bei jeder Begegnung mit einem asiatischen Geschäftsmann **überreichen Sie** zuerst **Ihre Visitenkarte**. Das wird erwartet und begrüßt. Von da an sind Sie auf sich selbst gestellt, solange Sie daran denken, die ganze Zeit über höflich und ehrerbietig zu sein. Zeigen Sie niemals Ungeduld, Gereiztheit oder Ärger. Das wird zu nichts führen.

P. Will there be many participants from Asia at the conference?

P. Werden viele Teilnehmer aus Asien bei der Konferenz dabei sein?

C. Oh yes, quite a few. I don't know if you class Russia as Asia, but Moscow is sending a very **high-level delegation**.

C. Oh ja, eine ganze Menge. Ich weiß nicht, ob Sie Russland zu Asien zählen, aber Moskau schickt eine **hochkarätige Delegation**.

P. And how can you describe the best way of **doing business with Russians**?

P. Und was ist Ihrer Meinung nach die beste Art, **mit Russen Geschäfte zu machen**?

C. Forget the past – you're dealing with a completely new generation and a totally new set of standards. Being a German, you would have no difficulty dealing with Russians. They are **highly-motivated**, **innovative** and **progressive** business people. But let's take a look now at the agenda. I don't want to take up more of your time than necessary. You must be a very busy man ...

C. Vergessen Sie die Vergangenheit – Sie verhandeln mit einer völlig neuen Generation und ganz neuen Grundsätzen. Als Deutscher hätten Sie keine Schwierigkeit, mit Russen zu verhandeln. Sie sind **hoch motivierte**, **innovative** und **progressive** Geschäftsleute. Aber lassen Sie uns jetzt einen Blick auf die Tagesordnung werfen. Ich möchte nicht mehr von Ihrer Zeit in Anspruch nehmen als nötig. Sie müssen ein sehr beschäftigter Mann sein ...

Background Information

There are undeniably differences to be observed in **business dealings** with people from distinct regions of the world, such as Asia. But **clichés** and, of course, **prejudices** should be avoided at all costs. A **correct appearance**, **politeness**, **consideration for a competitor's point of view** are invariably sufficient in any business situation. And, of course, business cards – not only in encounters with Asian business people.

Train Yourself

Ever or never?

Mr Carter advises Peter »never, ever« to show impatience, irritation or particularly anger in dealings with Asian business people. He could have said just »never«, but the use of »ever« strengthens his recommendation. **Fill the gaps in the following sentences with »ever« or »never«:**

1. Did you ________ see that film I recommended?
2. Have you ________ been to Paris? I can hardly believe it.
3. Did you ________ see such a thing in your life?
4. Well, I ________! I ________ expected to see the Smiths at this party.
5. She says that she's happier than ________ before now that she's married.
6. I'm ________ so pleased to see Tom as when he's sober.
7. I'm ________ so pleased to meet you at last, John.
8. They're ________ the wiser for the dreadful time they had on their last trip to Africa. They're going back there on holiday next year.

Talk Talk Talk

P. Hello Lucy. **Any messages for me?**	P. Hallo Lucy. **Irgendwelche Nachrichten für mich?**
L. Yes, a Mr Atherton-Smith called.	L. Ja, ein Mr Atherton-Smith hat angerufen.
P. Atherton-Smythe? Good old Archie? What did he say?	P. Atherton-Smythe? Der gute alte Archie? Was hat er gesagt?
L. He'll **call back** later this afternoon.	L. Er wird im Laufe des Nachmittags **noch einmal anrufen**.
P. He didn't **leave a number**?	P. Hat er keine **Nummer hinterlassen**?
L. No, he said he was **running from one appointment to another** and didn't know where he'd be when you got back. He also said	L. Nein, er sagte, er würde **von einer Verabredung zur nächsten rasen** und wüsste nicht, wo er sein würde, wenn Sie zurückkommen.

that unfortunately, he wasn't available on his mobile these days either.

Er sagte auch, dass er zurzeit leider auch nicht auf seinem Handy erreichbar ist.

P. OK, I'll wait for his call ...
Why, hello Steve! Long time no see, as you say. How are you? How's life?

P. In Ordnung, ich werde auf seinen Anruf warten ...
Ja! Hallo Steve! Lange nicht gesehen, wie man sagt. Wie geht es Ihnen? Was macht das Leben?

S. Peter! Hi! Good to see you again. How was New York? James has really put me through it. It seems the company just can't keep up with business now and we've really got to get down to some hard slogging. It's **all hands to the wheel**. **What are you up to** at the moment? OK, you can tell me over a glass. Lucy, when Mr Morgan comes back tell him Peter here and I are having a late lunch or an early cocktail hour – I don't mind which.

S. Peter! Hi! Schön, Sie wieder zu sehen. Wie war New York? James hat mich wirklich hart rangenommen. Es scheint, als könnte die Firma gerade nicht mit dem Geschäft mithalten und wir müssen wirklich hart schuften. Es heißt **alle Mann ans Ruder**. **Woran arbeiten Sie** gerade? In Ordnung, das können Sie mir bei einem Drink erzählen. Lucy, wenn Mr Morgan zurückkommt, sagen Sie ihm, Peter und ich nehmen ein spätes Mittagessen oder einen frühen Cocktail ein – egal was.

L. And Mr what's-his-name, Mr Brückner?

L. Und Mr »Wie-hieß-er-noch-mal«, Mr Brückner?

P. Atherton-Smythe, Lucy. If he calls tell him we're at the Bleke Street wine bar if he happens to be in the area anytime in the next hour or so.

P. Atherton-Smythe, Lucy. Wenn er anruft, sagen Sie ihm bitte, wir sind im Weinlokal in der Bleke Street, falls er in der nächsten Stunde oder so zufällig in der Gegend ist.

S. Hour or so? It'll take you longer than that to tell me what you got

S. Stunde oder so? Sie werden länger als das brauchen, um mir

up to in New York. A little bird told me a certain young lady with the **initials** MW was there, too. How did you arrange that?

zu erzählen, was Sie in New York getrieben haben. Ein Vögelchen hat mir gezwitschert, dass eine gewisse junge Dame mit den **Initialen** MW auch dort war. Wie haben Sie das angestellt?

P. Steve, I know you're not going to believe this, but it was sheer coincidence.

P. Steve, ich weiß, Sie werden mir das nicht glauben, aber das war purer Zufall.

S. Oh come on, **tell me another**!

S. Ach kommen Sie schon, **Sie können mir viel erzählen**!

Background Information

Rumour plays as big a role in British life as anywhere else, and the English language has at least three very expressive ways of describing how this information – or, often, misinformation – is passed on:

A little bird told me she's got a new boyfriend.
That new company is on the verge of bankruptcy – I heard it on the grapevine.
I've heard on the bush telegraph that Charles and Mary are splitting up.
People who pass on information secretively in this way are called »rumourmongers«.

Train Yourself

Up and down

Steve asks Peter what he's up to at the moment – he asks him what he is doing, what job or task he's involved in. Steve says all at Ergo have to get down to some hard slogging, meaning they have to devote themselves to some hard work. **In the following sentences complete the expressions using »up« and »down« with, where applicable, the correct verb and preposition:**

1. I don't know what Pete (*get*) __________ last night, but this morning he looks very tired indeed.
2. When it (*come*) __________ to it, all that matters to John is good health and a happy home life.
3. Mary is really __________ heart after being jilted so suddenly like that.
4. I like your suggestion, it suits me __________ the ground.
5. The boss is very much __________ that new employee, he doesn't like him at all.
6. You have presented us with a very difficult problem here. I can't remember ever (*be*) __________ anything so complicated.

Talk Talk Talk

(The Bleke Street wine bar)	(Das Bleke Street Weinlokal)
S. Shall we **split** a bottle of that excellent Nuits St. George?	S. Sollen wir uns eine Flasche dieses exzellenten Nuits St. George **teilen**?
P. **Fine by me**, Steve.	P. **Gerne**, Steve.
S. James Morgan obviously has plans for you, my friend. You'll be in government before long, **mark my words**.	S. James Morgan hat offensichtlich Pläne mit Ihnen, mein Freund. Über kurz oder lang werden Sie in der Regierung sitzen, **denken Sie an meine Worte**.
P. You forget two important things, Steve. I'm German. And I'm not at all interested in politics. Ergo is my life at the moment.	P. Steve, Sie vergessen zwei wichtige Dinge. Ich bin Deutscher. Und ich bin überhaupt nicht an Politik interessiert. Ergo ist derzeit mein Leben.
S. And is no one likely to be sharing that life soon?	S. Und wird niemand dieses Leben bald teilen?

P. You mean Melissa? Look, let me tell you about a very embarrassing **occurrence** in New York that seems to have **scuppered** any chances I had with Melissa ...

P. Sie meinen Melissa? Passen Sie auf, lassen Sie mich von einem sehr unangenehmen **Vorfall** in New York berichten, der alle Chancen **ruiniert** hat, die ich bei Melissa hatte ...

P. Hi, Archie! How good to see you again! You **got the message** I left at the office? Come, join us in a glass of this excellent wine. Steve, this is the Archie I've been telling you about. Archie, **this is my colleague** and good friend Steve Blackman.

P. He, Archie! Wie schön, Sie wieder zu sehen! Sie haben die **Nachricht bekommen**, die ich im Büro hinterlassen habe? Kommen Sie, leisten Sie uns Gesellschaft bei einem Glas dieses ausgezeichneten Weins. Steve, das ist der Archie, von dem ich Ihnen erzählt habe. Archie, **dies** ist **mein Kollege** und guter Freund Steve Blackman.

A-S. **I'm very pleased to make your acquaintance.** Any friend of Peter's is a friend of mine. Have you settled back into life in Britain after your time in New York, Peter?

A-S. **Sehr erfreut, Ihre Bekanntschaft zu machen.** Jeder Freund von Peter ist auch ein Freund von mir. Peter, haben Sie sich nach Ihrer Zeit in New York wieder eingelebt in das britische Leben?

P. No problem, Archie. I think I'm a European at heart.

P. Kein Problem, Archie. Ich glaube ich bin ein waschechter Europäer.

A-S. Well, I certainly am. I like the Americans and I like and admire their country, but I just can't keep up with their pace of life. I **ran for cover** immediately after I got back and made for my place in Buckinghamshire. Been there for the past few days. Peter, that's the real reason I called you. I'm having a house party next weekend. **Can**

A-S. Nun, das bin ich sicherlich. Ich mag die Amerikaner und ich mag und bewundere ihr Land, aber ich kann einfach nicht mit ihrem Lebensrhythmus mithalten. Ich **brachte mich** sofort **in Sicherheit**, als ich zurück war und machte mich auf den Weg zu meinem Haus in Buckinghamshire. Dort bin ich die letzten paar Tage gewesen.

you make it? Your friend, too, of course, if he cares to.

Peter, das ist der eigentliche Grund, weshalb ich Sie angerufen hatte. Nächstes Wochenende gebe ich eine Hausparty. **Können Sie das einrichten?** Ihr Freund ist natürlich auch eingeladen, wenn er möchte.

S. That's very kind of you, but I have to return to Glasgow **at the double**, now Peter's **back in harness**.

S. Das ist sehr nett von Ihnen, aber ich muss jetzt **doppelt so schnell** nach Glasgow zurückkehren, jetzt wo Peter **wieder in der Tretmühle** ist.

P. **I'd certainly like to come**, Archie. But first let's talk about how you got on in New York. **I hope the trip was worth it for you and your company** ...

P. **Ich komme natürlich gerne**, Archie. Aber zuerst einmal lassen Sie uns darüber sprechen, wie es Ihnen in New York ergangen ist. **Ich hoffe, die Reise hat sich für Sie und Ihre Firma gelohnt** ...

Background Information

1. The British probably **conclude more business deals** in **social encounters** than in the **formal surroundings of offices**. One economics researcher has estimated that deals worth nearly one billion pounds sterling a year are reached on British golf courses alone! Restaurants, bars and clubs also witness big business at work within their walls. And it's certain that Archie's country house party will be more than just an occasion for sampling bottles from his wine cellar!

2. Steve says jocularly that Peter has a future in politics, adding: **»Mark my words«**. There are several everyday expressions using »mark«, some of them especially useful in business situations:

to lose one's mark	to miss the chance of doing business
to make one's mark	to make a favourable impression

to mark down	to reduce the price
markdown	the amount by which a retail price is reduced
markup	the amount added to the cost of a product in order to reach a profitable retail price; the gross profit
to mark time	to remain stationary but in readiness (from the military term describing the action of marching on the spot without advancing)
on the mark	accurate
on your marks	under starter's orders in a race: »On your marks, get set, go!«
up to the mark	up to standard, satisfactory (usually used in the negative)

Train Yourself

Select the correct words and expressions using »mark« in the following sentences:

1. She quickly __________ in the office and won rapid promotion.
2. Your calculation of the __________ on that new product was very accurate, right __________.
3. His work performance has not been very satisfactory lately, he's not been at all __________.
4. The runners are __________, and they're off!
5. After an impressive run of success, the company appears to have ground to a standstill and to be __________.
6. They could so easily have sealed that deal but by holding out for a higher price they __________.
7. If they had only __________ the retail price by as little as ten percent they might not have __________.
8. The __________ the company expects to achieve on that new line is far too high.

Talk Talk Talk

(Ministry of Overseas Trade)

Under-Secretary Carter: Ah, Mr Brückner! Welcome, welcome! How good to see you again. This way, please. The Minister is **receiving guests** in the **conference room** ... Minister, this is Mr Brückner – but I'm sure you remember him.

M. Yes, indeed. Thank you so much for agreeing to attend, Mr Brückner. **I value your participation highly.**

P. I'm honoured to have been invited, Minister.

M. We'll be getting under way shortly, but please **let me introduce you to** the President of the Central and South American Trade Organization, Rodrigo Jaime de Calares. Señor Jaime, **may I introduce** Mr Peter Brückner of Ergo Limited. Mr Brückner is a **shining example** of what we were just talking about – the necessity **of crossborder**, practical integration of **nonnational business acumen**. Mr Brückner, you see, is German but working for a British concern which is now expanding into the

(Außenhandelsministerium)

Staatssektretär Carter: Ah, Mr Brückner! Willkommen, willkommen! Wie schön, Sie wieder zu sehen. Bitte hier entlang. Der Minister **empfängt** gerade die **Gäste** im **Konferenzraum** ... Herr Minister, das ist Mr Brückner – aber ich bin sicher, Sie erinnern sich an ihn.

M. Ja, in der Tat. Vielen Dank, dass Sie sich bereit erklärt haben, beizuwohnen, Mr Brückner. **Ich schätze Ihre Teilnahme sehr.**

P. Es ist mir eine Ehre, eingeladen worden zu sein, Herr Minister.

M. Nun, wir werden in Kürze beginnen, doch **lassen Sie mich Sie** dem Präsidenten der Handelsorganisation von Zentral- und Südamerika, Rodrigo Jaime de Calares, **vorstellen**. Señor Jaime, **darf ich vorstellen**, Peter Brückner von Ergo Limited. Mr Brückner ist ein **leuchtendes Beispiel** dafür, worüber wir gerade gesprochen haben – die Notwendigkeit der **Grenzüberschreitung**, praktische Integration von **nicht-nationalem Geschäftsscharfsinn**. Sehen Sie, Mr Brückner ist Deutscher, arbeitet

North American market. He is a living example of one of the **chief items on our agenda** here. I hope you don't mind being described in those terms, Mr Brückner?

aber für einen britischen Konzern, der jetzt auf dem nordamerikanischen Markt expandiert. Er ist ein lebendes Beispiel für einen der **Hauptpunkte auf unserer Tagesordnung** hier. Ich hoffe, es stört Sie nicht, anhand dieser Begriffe beschrieben zu werden, Mr Brückner?

P. Well, I'm not sure if I grasped the full meaning of the role you have given me, but I have complete faith in your judgment, of course, Minister.

P. Nun, ich bin mir nicht sicher, ob ich die ganze Bedeutung der Rolle, die Sie mir gegeben haben, erfasst habe, aber ich habe natürlich völliges Vertrauen in Ihr Urteilsvermögen, Herr Minister.

M. Then **let me leave you with** Señor Jaime while I prepare for the opening of the conference.

M. Dann **lasse ich Sie jetzt mit** Señor Jaime **allein**, während ich mich auf die Eröffnung der Konferenz vorbereite.

J. Do you know Central or South America, Mr Brückner?

J. Kennen Sie Zentral- oder Südamerika, Mr Brückner?

P. Unfortunately not. In fact, I've only just returned from my first visit to North America.

P. Leider nicht. Eigentlich bin ich gerade erst von meinem ersten Besuch in Nordamerika zurückgekehrt.

J. I think you'd feel very much at home in my country, Argentina, and anywhere else in the region. We very much **value** the **German style of doing business**.

J. Ich glaube, Sie würden sich in Argentinien, meiner Heimat, sehr wohl fühlen und überall sonst in der Region. Wir **schätzen die deutsche Art, Geschäfte zu machen**, sehr.

P. And that is?

P. Und das ist?

J. Hard, direct – but always cor-

J. Hart, direkt – aber immer korrect. You say no, you mean no. When you say yes we know we have a **contract**. In our region yes can often mean no. We hate to say no – but that is a very bad **trait** in business.

rekt. Wenn sie Nein sagen, dann meinen sie auch Nein. Wenn sie Ja sagen, wissen wir, dass wir einen **Vertrag** haben. In unserer Region kann Ja oft Nein bedeuten. Wir hassen es, Nein zu sagen – aber das ist bei Geschäften ein sehr schlechter **Charakterzug**.

P. Yes – I mean no. Oh dear, Señor Jaime, I think you've confused me a bit there.

P. Ja – ich meine nein. Oh je, Señor Jaime, ich glaube, da haben Sie mich ein bisschen durcheinander gebracht.

J. Another Latin American **tactic** – ah, but **the conference is about to start**. I shall explain everything later, but I am not promising you will understand ...

J. Eine weitere lateinamerikanische **Taktik** – ah, aber **die Konferenz fängt gleich an**. Ich werde später alles erklären, aber ich verspreche Ihnen nicht, dass Sie es verstehen werden ...

Background Information

In **business dealings** in Spain, Central and South America don't be caught out by the flamboyant enthusiasm of Spanish farewells. »Hasta pronto« (»See you shortly«) does not mean you will be invited back the following day to seal a deal – treat all Spanish forms of farewell (»Hasta entonces«, »hasta luego«, »hasta la vista«) as versions of »Auf Wiedersehen« and you won't be disappointed by false hopes.

Train Yourself

Tenses

Peter says he has only just returned from the United States, using the present perfect form to describe an action or state of being so recent that it effectively continues in the present. **Select the correct form of**

the verb in brackets to use in the following sentences. Choose from the following tenses: past tense, present perfect, past perfect.

1. The company recently __________ (*set up*) a branch office in Glasgow to serve the Scottish market.
2. I __________ (*be*) in London now for several months, but I still __________ (not have) the time to tour the city's sights.
3. Jane told me she __________ (*be*) to Paris only once in her life. She __________ (go) when she was a student.
4. He told me he __________ (*have*) a terrible time when he __________ (go) to Russia last year.
5. They both __________ (*fall*) ill with food poisoning after they __________ (visit) that new seafood restaurant on the harbourside.
6. He just called to say he __________ (*fall*) ill and won't be able to complete the job of work he __________ (*start*) last month.
7. They __________ (*not leave*) yet? When we called a couple of hours ago we were told they __________ (*set off*) already.
8. I can't remember when I __________ (*be*) last in London. I __________ (*not visit*) the city for many years.

Talk Talk Talk

(Ergo offices, London)

(Ergo-Büros, London)

J. Peter, **how did the Ministry conference go**? I've already had a call from the Ministry to thank us for sending you. The Minister appears to have been very pleased by your **attendance**.

J. Peter, **wie ist die Außenhandelskonferenz gelaufen**? Ich habe schon einen Anruf vom Ministerium erhalten, um uns zu danken, dass wir Sie geschickt haben. Der Minister scheint von Ihrer **Teilnahme** sehr erfreut gewesen zu sein.

P. I found it very **instructive** and felt honoured to meet government representatives and business people from so many different countries. I **made** what might for us be

P. Ich fand sie sehr **lehrreich** und fühlte mich sehr geehrt, Regierungsverteter und Geschäftsleute aus so vielen verschiedenen Ländern zu treffen. Ich habe einen

a very **useful contact** with the President of the Central and South American Trade Organization.

Kontakt geknüpft, der für uns sehr **nützlich** sein könnte, mit dem Präsidenten der Handelsorganisation von Zentral- und Südamerika.

J. **Good for you!** Why don't you take off early for the weekend? You must be **all in** after all this hectic activity.

J. **Gut gemacht!** Warum gehen Sie nicht frühzeitig ins Wochenende? Sie müssen **ganz erledigt** sein, nach all der hektischen Aktivitäten.

P. I was about to ask you if you would mind if I **took** this afternoon **off**. I've been invited to a weekend at a friend's place in the country.

P. Ich wollte Sie gerade fragen, ob Sie etwas dagegen hätten, wenn ich mir heute Nachmittag **freinehme**. Ich bin über das Wochenende auf den Landsitz eines Freundes eingeladen.

J. **By all means**, Peter. Where is this place?

J. **Aber natürlich**, Peter. Wo ist dieser Landsitz?

P. Somewhere in Buckinghamshire. I have to find out first how to get there.

P. Irgendwo in Buckinghamshire. Ich muss erst noch herausfinden, wie man da hinkommt.

J. Lovely county, and I'm sure you'll have a great time. Just the time of year for some shooting. Does your friend shoot?

J. Schöne Grafschaft, und ich bin sicher, Sie werden eine tolle Zeit verbringen. Gerade die richtige Jahreszeit zum Jagen. Jagt Ihr Freund?

P. I don't think so. His hobby seems to be his wine cellar.

P. Das glaube ich nicht. Sein Weinkeller scheint sein Hobby zu sein.

J. You lucky chap – you'll at least be **well stocked** in that quarter ...

J. Sie Glückspilz – Sie werden zumindest diesbezüglich **gut versorgt** werden ...

(Walsingham Manor, Buckinghamshire)

(Walsingham Manor, Buckinghamshire)

P. This must be the place. Through these gates, please.

P. Das muss das Haus sein. Durch diese Tore, bitte.

Taxidriver: This is quite a pile, guv. Your pal a millionaire or something? Rock star perhaps?

Taxifahrer: Ganz schön großer Kasten, Chef! Ist Ihr Freund ein Millionär oder so etwas? Vielleicht Rockstar?

P. No. He's in **banking**.

P. Nein, er ist im **Bankwesen** tätig.

A-S. Peter, my dear boy. Welcome, welcome. Leave the taxi to me. Eight pounds? Here's ten, my good man. Thank you for delivering my good friend safe and sound ...

A-S. Peter, mein lieber Junge. Willkommen, willkommen. Überlassen Sie mir das Taxi. Acht Pfund? Hier sind zehn, guter Mann. Danke, dass Sie meinen Freund gut und wohlbehalten hier abgeliefert haben ...

Train Yourself

Multiple choice

Let's take a little time now to revise some of the expressions using the verb »take«. **Select the correct preposition to use in the following sentences:**

1. He took ______ a very difficult task when he accepted that job (*up, on, with, to*).
2. She took ______ him from their first meeting, and how they are married (*up, on, to, over*).
3. They didn't perform that job very well and were thoroughly taken ______ task by the boss (*to, up, on, over*).
4. The salesman really took them ______ a ride by selling them that beaten-up car for three thousand pounds (*on, over, with, for*).
5. He feels his abilities aren't being properly recognized and believes he is being taken ______ granted (*with, on, for, by*).

6. I don't think it's very fair to take her name ________ vain like that (*for, in, at, under*).
7. You look so much like my friend John I could have taken you ________ his brother (*as, to, for, at*).
8. It's the president's turn to speak next, he'll shortly be taking (*up, –, on, over*) the floor.

Talk Talk Talk

A-S. You're just in time for a cocktail before dinner. Most of the other guests are here. Alfred! Take Mr Brückner's coat and hat, please. Alfred is my new butler, but he's rather ancient and slow.

A-S. Sie kommen gerade richtig zu einem Cocktail vor dem Abendessen. Die meisten der anderen Gäste sind hier. Alfred! Nehmen Sie bitte Mr Brückners Mantel und Hut. Alfred ist mein neuer Butler, aber er ist ziemlich alt und langsam.

P. A butler! Archie, you do live well.

P. Ein Butler! Archie, Sie leben aber gut.

A-S. Not as well as my grandfather, who left me this little place and the company. My father, God rest his soul, frittered a lot away at cards and on the racecourse. I'm trying to claw it all back ... Ah, here's the man who is helping me. My **financial adviser**, Solomon Gold – his name sums him up, he's **worth his weight in gold** to me. Sol, you old rascal, meet my friend Peter Brückner. Peter, this is Solomon Gold. If you need **advice** in any financial matter turn to him.

A-S. Nicht so gut wie mein Großvater, der mir dieses kleine Haus und die Firma hinterlassen hat. Mein Vater, Gott gebe seiner Seele Frieden, hat eine Menge beim Karten spielen und auf der Rennbahn verplempert. Ich versuche, mir alles zurückzukrallen ... Ah, da ist der Mann, der mir dabei hilft. Mein **Finanzberater**, Solomon Gold – sein Name sagt alles, für mich ist er **sein Gewicht in Gold wert**. Sol, Sie alter Schurke, lernen Sie meinen Freund Peter Brückner kennen. Peter, das ist Solomon Gold. Wenn Sie in irgendeiner finanziellen Angelegenheit **Rat** brauchen, wenden Sie sich an ihn.

S. Oh, I haven't always been so reliable with that advice as I've proved with you, Archie. Peter, I'm delighted to meet you ...

S. Oh, ich bin nicht immer so verlässlich mit diesem Rat gewesen, wie ich mich bei Ihnen erwiesen habe, Archie. Peter, es freut mich, Sie kennen zu lernen ...

A-S. And over here, Peter, is James Duvall – do you remember him from New York? The film producer Duvall? He's come – to look my little place over as a possible location for that costume drama he was telling us about.

A-S. Und hier drüben, Peter, ist James Duvall – erinnern Sie sich an ihn von New York her? Der Filmproduzent Duvall? Er ist gekommen, um zu sehen, ob mein bescheidenes Zuhause als möglicher Platz für diesen Kostümfilm, von dem er uns erzählt hat, in Frage kommt.

JD. And to look you over too, Archie. I think I might have a good role for you. Hello, Peter! Good to see you again.

JD. Und auch, um bei Ihnen vorbeizuschauen, Archie. Ich glaube, ich hätte da eine gute Rolle für Sie. Hallo Peter! Schön, Sie wieder zu sehen.

A-S. Peter, I've got somebody here who'll make you even more nostalgic. See that pretty girl over there by the fireplace?

A-S. Peter, es ist jemand hier, der Sie sogar noch nostalgischer stimmen wird. Sehen Sie das hübsche Mädchen da drüben am Kamin?

P. Why yes, but it can't be – can it?

P. Aber ja, aber das kann nicht sein – oder?

A-S. Melissa! Come here, my dear! Look who's come for dinner!

A-S. Melissa! Kommen Sie her, meine Liebe! Sehen Sie mal, wer zum Essen kommt!

M. Peter!

M. Peter!

P. Melissa! But how ...?

P. Melissa! Aber wie ...?

A-S. Has nothing to do with you, dear boy. Melissa has **taken over** the Royal Star Banking **account**. She's in England to **acquaint herself with the operation** and then, because of her near-fluent German, is off to Germany next week to **look at co-operation possibilities** there.	A-S. Hat nichts mit Ihnen zu tun, mein Lieber. Melissa hat die Royal Star Banking als **Kunden übernommen**. Sie ist in England, um **sich mit der Operation vertraut** zu **machen**. Und dann fährt sie wegen ihres beinahe fließenden Deutsch nächste Woche nach Deutschland, um sich dort **nach Kooperationsmöglichkeiten umzusehen**.
P. Melissa, I left New York without clearing up that misunderstanding at Tiffany's.	P. Melissa, ich verließ New York, ohne das Missverständnis bei Tiffany's aufzuklären.
M. You don't have to explain, Peter. Archie told me the whole story.	M. Sie müssen nichts erklären, Peter. Archie hat mir die ganze Geschichte erzählt.
P. And now you're off to Germany?	P. Und jetzt sind Sie auf dem Weg nach Deutschland?
M. To Dresden.	M. Nach Dresden.
P. I'm going back to Hamburg next week for Christmas and New Year. But I know Dresden very well. My family is originally from Saxony.	P. Ich fahre nächste Woche zu Weihnachten und Neujahr nach Hamburg zurück. Aber ich kenne Dresden sehr gut. Meine Familie kommt ursprünglich aus Sachsen.
M. I'm told Christmas is a lovely time to be there.	M. Man sagt, zu Weihnachten ist es dort sehr schön.
P. Dresden has a wonderful Christmas market. May I show it to you? Dresden is just a few hours from Hamburg by train.	P. Dresden hat einen wunderschönen Weihnachtsmarkt. Darf ich ihn Ihnen zeigen? Dresden ist mit dem Zug nur ein paar Stunden von Hamburg entfernt.

M. This is where we came in isn't it, Peter? A train journey? Just don't let Steve buy the tickets ...

M. So haben wir angefangen, nicht wahr, Peter? Eine Bahnfahrt? Aber lassen Sie bloß Steve nicht die Fahrscheine kaufen ...

And so we say farewell to Peter, Melissa and their friends.

Und so verabschieden wir uns von Peter, Melissa und ihren Freunden.

Vocabulary

account	hier: Kunde, auch Bericht, Rechnung, Konto
to acquaint oneself with the operation	sich mit der Operation vertraut machen
agenda	Tagesordnung
all hands to the wheel	alle Mann an die Ruder
to approach a meeting	an eine Verhandlung herangehen
Asian business market	asiatischer Geschäftsmarkt
at all costs	um jeden Preis
attendance	Teilnahme
back in harness	wieder in der Tretmühle
banking	Bankwesen
to be all in	völlig erledigt sein
break into the Asian market	in den asiatischen Markt eindringen
by all means	aber natürlich
to call back	zurückrufen
Can you make it?	Können Sie das einrichten? (Verabredung)
chief items	Hauptpunkte
conference room	Konferenzraum
contact	Kontakt
cross-border	Grenzüberschreitung
to deal in American markets	auf amerikanischen Märkten verhandeln
differences in approach	Unterschiede in der Handlungsweise/Methode
difficult market	schwieriger Markt

doing business with ...	mit ... Geschäfte machen
fine by me	gerne
foreign experience	Auslandserfahrung
foreign expert	Auslandsexperte
to get the message	die Nachricht erhalten
Good for you!	Gut gemacht!
to hang on to	dran bleiben
to hate to lose face	es hassen, das Gesicht zu verlieren
to have an appointment	eine Verabredung haben
high-level delegation	hochkarätige Delegation/ Abordnung
highly-motivated	hoch motiviert
How did the conference go?	Wie ist die Konferenz gelaufen?
I'm very pleased to make your acquaintance.	Sehr erfreut, Ihre Bekanntschaft zu machen.
initials	Initialen
innovative	innovativ
instructive	lehrreich
international arena	internationaler Schauplatz
laid back	relaxed
to leave a number	eine Nummer hinterlassen
to look at co-operation possibilities	sich nach Kooperationsmöglichkeiten umsehen
to make useful contact with	einen nützlichen Kontakt knüpfen mit
Mark my words!	Denken Sie an meine Worte!
May I introduce ...	Darf ich vorstellen ...
message	Nachricht
multinational conference	multinationale Konferenz
non-national business acumen	nichtnationaler Geschäftsscharfsinn
occurrence	Vorfall
practical knowledge	praktische Erfahrung
to present one's business card	seine Visitenkarte überreichen
progressive	progressiv, fortschrittlich
to run for cover	sich in Sicherheit bringen, verstecken

to run from one appointment to another	von einer Verabredung zur nächsten rasen
shining example	leuchtendes Beispiel
to sign the book	im Buch unterschreiben
to split	teilen
tactic	Taktik
to take off	sich freinehmen
to take over	übernehmen
Tell me another!	Sie können mir viel erzählen!
The conference is about to start.	Die Konferenz fängt gleich an.
This is my colleague.	Dies ist mein Kollege.
trait	Charakterzug
visitor's pass	Besucherausweis
well stocked	gut versorgt
What are you up to?	Woran arbeiten Sie gerade?/Was machen Sie gerade?
worth his (her) weight in gold	sein (ihr) Gewicht in Gold wert sein

The Test – how good are you now at conversation?

1. Complete the following sentences, using words chosen from those given in parentheses:

a. How do you do? I'm very ______ to meet you (*proud, relieved, pleased, honoured*).

b. She has fully recovered from the operation? I ______ (*must, can't, can, have to*) tell you how ______ (*exhausted, relieved, disappointed, honoured*) I am.

c. Please ______ (*pass on to, tell, inform, assure*) your father how ______ (*sad, dismayed, surprised, shocked*) I was to hear of his wife's death.

d. Jane's getting married? Give her my ______ (*commiseration, sympathy, joy, best wishes*).

e. Please tell Mr Johnson how ______ (*overjoyed, pleased, surprised, encouraged*) I was to hear of his promotion. Oh, and give him my ______ (*sympathy, fine feelings, good wishes, encouragement*) for the future.

f. ______ me (*Forgive, Listen to, Excuse, Hear*)! Is this seat ______ (*promised, taken, used, paid for*)?

g. Good morning, Polly! Could you tell Mr Smithers I shan't be in today? I'm feeling ______ (*down-at-heart, down, off-putting, off-colour*).

h. Fill your glasses, please! I would like to ______ (*say, give, propose, honour*) a toast to the happy couple!

i. In ______,(*replying, reflection, response, answer*) I ______ (*have, want, desire, don't hesitate*) to say how happy I have been working for this company.

j. May I break ________ (*out, in, down, up*) on this conversation? You can count ________ (*in, down, on, up*) my support for what you are proposing.

2. When you wish to convey your sympathy in the case of somebody's death you offer your *condolences.* **What expressions do you offer in the following events?**

a. Announcement of an engagement or marriage?

b. A friend's promotion at work?

c. Farewell to friends embarking on a long journey?

d. ... and on a short journey?

e. A run of bad luck experienced by a friend?

f. Failure by a friend to honour a promise?

g. A road accident in which a friend is injured?

h. Assistance afforded by a friend?

And the possibilities: *Expressions of ...*

disappointment, anger, delight, good wishes, concern, empathy, dismay, encouragement, thanks, good luck wishes, congratulations, sympathy, Good speed!

3. Have you mastered those prepositions? **Choose the correct ones to employ with the expressions used in the following sentences, selecting them from those given in parentheses:**

a. This is supposed to be a secret, so don't let ________ (*up, down, on, in*) to John what we have ________ (*on, under, in, at*) mind.

b. How long can the company keep this progress __________ (*on, in, up, down*)? I hope we shareholders are informed __________ (*on, at, in, around*) time if a reversal is expected.

c. You can't keep a good man __________ (*in, down, up, under*). Smith's talent will show __________ (*at, on, in, down*) the end.

d. I wish I knew what this speaker is getting __________ (*at, on, for, down*), he seems quite __________ (*on, off, at, under*) the mark.

e. Janet says they made that story __________ (*down, up, on, off*) just to get __________ (*at, on, over, down on*) us.

f. We're all __________ (*down, up, in, out*) after a very heavy week at work, in fact I'm done __________ (*out, in, over, under*).

g. I'd like to know what they're up __________ (*on, over, to, from*). Can you sound them __________ (*down, over, in, out*) for me?

h. When that department finally gets down __________ (*on, over, to, from*) it we can count __________ (*out, on, over, at*) some promising results.

i. You can always count __________ (*in, for, with, on*) the company's personnel department if you're in trouble.

j. We had to bring __________ (*on, up, in, down*) an independent company of accountants to look __________ (*at, over, into, up*) the mysterious loss of so much money.

Ready to talk

1. Auf Konferenzen

Can you tell me where I register, please?	Wo kann ich mich anmelden?
Excuse me, where is the conference room?	Entschuldigung, wo finde ich den Konferenzraum?
I'd like to pick up my registration pack.	Ich möchte meine Konferenzmappe abholen.
You wouldn't happen to have ...?	Sie haben nicht zufällig ...?
Would you please fill in the registration form?	Könnten Sie bitte dieses Anmeldeformular ausfüllen?
For some reason you're not on the list.	Aus irgendeinem Grund stehen Sie nicht auf der Liste.
Excuse me, you've spelt my name wrong.	Entschuldigung, aber Sie haben meinen Namen falsch buchstabiert.
I need ... How can that be arranged?	Ich brauche ... Könnten Sie das veranlassen?
Where do I sign up for ...?	Wo kann ich mich für ... eintragen?
It's my pleasure to welcome you all to the conference.	Es freut mich, Sie alle auf unserer Konferenz begrüßen zu dürfen.
It's my pleasure to introduce our first speaker, Mr Morgan, who will be talking about ...	Es freut mich, unseren ersten Redner, Mr Morgan, vorzustellen, der über ... sprechen wird.
Excuse me, don't we know one another by sight?	Entschuldigen Sie bitte, kennen wir uns nicht schon vom Sehen?
I think we've met before.	Ich glaube, wir sind uns schon einmal begegnet.
My name is ...	Mein Name ist .../Ich heiße ...
Could you tell me your name, please?	Wie ist Ihr Name bitte?
Pleased to meet you.	Freut mich, Sie kennen zu lernen.

Glad to meet you, too./The pleasure is mine.	Ganz meinerseits.
Mr Atherton, may I introduce you to Ms Walker?	Mr Atherton, darf ich Ihnen Frau Walker vorstellen?
Peter, I'd like you to meet Amanda.	Peter, ich möchte dich mit Amanda bekannt machen.
Do you happen to know the guest speaker?	Kennen Sie vielleicht den Gastredner?
I wonder if I could borrow your copy of the agenda?	Könnte ich Ihre Kopie der Tagesordnung ausleihen?
Where do you work?/What company do you represent?	Wo arbeiten Sie/Welche Firma vertreten Sie?
What line are you in?	In welcher Branche sind Sie tätig?
Here's my card.	Hier ist meine Visitenkarte/Karte.
What do you expect form this conference?	Was erwarten Sie von dieser Konferenz?

2. Gesprächsanbahnung

Excuse me, Peter, can I have a word with you?	Entschuldigung, Peter, kann ich Sie kurz sprechen?
Have you got a moment Mr Brückner? I'd like to ask you a question.	Haben Sie einen Moment Zeit, Mr Brückner? Ich würde Sie gerne etwas fragen.
Peter, I've something important to discuss with you.	Peter, ich habe etwas Wichtiges mit dir zu besprechen.
Ms Walker, I'd really appreciate a moment of your time.	Ms Walker, ich wäre Ihnen sehr dankbar, wenn Sie einen Moment Zeit für mich hätten.

3. Geschäftsverbindungen knüpfen

Mr Brückner, you seem to know a lot about security in online business.	Mr Brückner, Sie scheinen ja eine ganze Menge über Sicherheit im Online-Business zu wissen.

Ms Walker, you seem to be an expert on ...	Ms Walker, Sie sind ja eine Expertin in ...
Archie mentioned that you might be able to recommend a good supplier for ...	Archie erwähnte, dass Sie mir eventuell einen guten Lieferanten für ... empfehlen können.
Mr Brückner, our business interests overlap in some areas.	Mr Brückner, unsere Geschäftsinteressen scheinen sich offensichtlich zu überschneiden.

4. Standpunkte vertreten und verteidigen

I think/believe that ...	Ich denke/meine, dass ...
If you ask me ...	Wenn Sie mich fragen, ...
I'm sure/persuaded that ...	Ich bin sicher/überzeugt, dass ...
From my point of view/In my view/In my opinion ...	Meiner Meinung nach ...
It's my conviction that ...	Ich bin überzeugt, dass ...
As far as I'm concerned, I think that ...	Was mich betrifft, so glaube ich, dass ...
Sorry to break in, but ...	Tut mir Leid, dass ich Sie unterbreche, aber ...
It's my firm belief that this is the best solution.	Ich bin der festen Überzeugung, dass dies die beste Lösung ist.
I'm afraid, I absolutely disagree with you.	Ich fürchte, ich bin ganz anderer Meinung als Sie.
Unfortunately, I can't share your point of view.	Ich kann Ihre Ansicht leider nicht teilen.
I've got some reservations.	Ich habe einige Bedenken.
To a certain extent I can agree with you.	Bis zu einem gewissen Grad kann ich Ihnen zustimmen.
To be honest, dont you think that my suggestion is more realistic?	Um ehrlich zu sein, glauben Sie nicht, dass mein Vorschlag realistischer ist?
I think you're on the wrong track.	Ich denke, Sie sind auf dem falschen Weg.
I doubt that you've considered everything.	Ich bezweifle, dass Sie alles in Betracht gezogen haben.

Glossary

a good grasp of something	etwas gut im Griff haben
to amalgamate	fusionieren, sich zusammenschließen
account	hier: Kunde, auch Bericht, Rechnung, Konto
to acquaint oneself with the operation	sich mit der Operation vertraut machen
address	Ansprache
advance copy	Vorabkopie
agenda	Tagesordnung
to allow	erlauben
annual holiday	Jahresurlaub
to approach a meeting	an eine Verhandlung herangehen
business market	Geschäftsmarkt
assistance	Unterstützung
assistant	Assistent, Stellvertreter
at all costs	um jeden Preis
at business	im Geschäft
at the double	doppelt so schnell
at your leisure	wenn es Ihnen passt
to attend (a conference, a meeting)	teilnehmen (an einer Konferenz, an einer Besprechung)
attendance	Teilnahme
back in harness	wieder in der Tretmühle
banking	Bankwesen
bank manager	Bankmanager
to bargain	verhandeln
to be accredited	akkreditiert sein
to be bound	sicher sein
to be in charge	verantworlich sein für
to be in marketing	im Marketing tätig sein
to be leaders in a field	führend sein auf einem Gebiet
to believe in a product	an ein Produkt glauben
to be one's area of business	das Geschäftsgebiet von jemandem sein

to break even	den „Break-Even-Point“ erreichen
to break into a market	in einen Markt eindringen
business plan	Geschäftsplan
business talks	Geschäftsgespräche
busy	beschäftigt
to call back	zurückrufen
Can you make it?	Können Sie das einrichten?
to catch up	aufholen
card	Visitenkarte
to charge	auf die Rechnung setzen
to chase	hinter etwas her sein, etw. verfolgen
to check it out	unter die Lupe nehmen
chief items	Hauptpunkte
client	Kunde
colleague	Kollege
commission charge	Provision
to come off it	mit etwas aufhören
to come through with flying colours	mit fliegenden Fahnen durchkommen/Erfolg haben
company	Unternehmen
competition	Konkurrenz
conference	Konferenz
conference on information technology	Informationstechnologie-Konferenz
conference room	Konferenzraum
conference venue	Konferenzort
conferencing	das Konferieren
contact	Kontakt
to cost a bomb	ein Vermögen kosten
credit card charges	hier: Kreditkartenbeträge
crew	Mannschaft
cross-border	Grenzüberschreitung
day's proceedings	Tagesverlauf
deal	Geschäft, Handel, Abmachung
to deal in semiconductors	mit Halbleitern handeln
dealing in American markets	auf amerikanischen Märkten verhandeln
description	Beschreibung

differences in approach	Unterschiede in der Handlungsweise/Methode
difficult market	schwieriger Markt
to discuss a possible co-operation	über eine mögliche Zusammen-arbeit sprechen
display of products	Produktpräsentation
diversification	Diversifikation/breiteres Angebot
to do business	Geschäfte machen
to drive a hard bargain	harte Verhandlungen führen
early customer	»früher Kunde«/früh dran sein, ein »Überpünktlicher«
e-commerce	E-Commerce
electronic communication	elektronische Kommunikation
electronics symposium	Elektronik-Symposium
embarrassment	Peinlichkeit, Verlegenheit
engagement book	Terminkalender
enterprise	Unternehmen
everything in one's power	alles in seiner Macht Stehende
to expand the network of contacts	das Netz von Kontakten erweitern
expansion	Expansion, Ausbreitung
expansion programme	Expansionsprogramm
experienced	erfahren, routiniert
export-import enterprise	Export-Import-Unternehmen
to extend	expandieren
factory	Fabrik
facts and figures	Fakten und Zahlen
to fail	versagen
favourable rate	Vorzugspreis
to fill one in	jemanden informieren
final session	Abschlusssitzung
financial backing	finanzielle Unterstützung
Fine by me.	Einverstanden.
to fit nicely	gut passen
flexible	flexibel
foreign experience	Auslandserfahrung
foreign expert	Auslandsexperte
for free	umsonst
to found	gründen

founder	Gründer
to get along	zurechtkommen, weiterkommen
to get done with	(etwas) erledigen
to get down to work	sich an die Arbeit machen
to get the message	die Nachricht erhalten
to get to grips with	sich mit (etwas) auseinandersetzen
to go into banking	sich dem Bankwesen widmen
to hang on to	dran bleiben
to hate to lose face	es hassen, das Gesicht zu verlieren
to have in mind	vorhaben
to have an appointment	eine Verabredung haben
head	Vorsitzender
headquarters	Hauptquartier
Here's my/his/her card.	Hier ist meine/seine/ihre (Visiten-)Karte.
high-level delegation	hochkarätige Delegation/ Abordnung
highly-motivated	hoch motiviert
high-tech	Hightech
How did the conference go?	Wie ist die Konferenz gelaufen?
How do you do?	Guten Tag.
I do hope we stay in contact.	Ich hoffe, wir bleiben in Kontakt.
I'd like to show you ...	Ich würde Ihnen gerne ... zeigen.
import-export business	Import-Export-Unternehmen
in all seriousness	ganz im Ernst
in business	beruflich
in good hands	in guten Händen
in profit	in der Profitzone
in return	im Gegenzug
in the market for	auf dem Markt sein mit
industrial actions	Arbeitskämpfe
information desk	Informationsschalter
information material	Informationsmaterial
information pack	Infopaket
information technology	Informationstechnologie
initials	Initialen
innovative	innovativ, Neuem aufgeschlossen

instructive	lehrreich
international arena	internationale Bühne
international forum	internationales Forum
to introduce somebody	jemanden vorstellen
to invest in	investieren in
investment	Investition
investment potential	Investitionspotenzial
IT boom	IT-Boom
to join somebody	sich zu jemandem setzen
to keep afloat	über Wasser halten
to keep one's appointment book clear	seinen Terminkalender freihalten
to keep to	etwas einhalten
to keep up	mithalten
knowledge	Kenntnisse
label	Etikett
labour-intensive	arbeitsaufwendig
large management staff	personalstarkes Management
large range of products	breite Palette an Produkten
line	Branche
to leave a number	eine Telefonnummer hinterlassen
logo	Logo
London-based company	Firma mit Sitz in London
to look at co-operation possibilities	sich nach Kooperationsmöglichkeiten umsehen
to look at the agenda	die Tagesordnung durchgehen
to look by	vorbeischauen
to make contact with	Kontakt aufnehmen mit
to make out	etwas hinstellen als, behaupten
to make record profits	gewaltige Gewinne machen
to make useful contact with	einen nützlichen Kontakt knüpfen mit
to manage	hinbekommen, schaffen
managing director	Geschäftsführer
manufacturer	Hersteller
mark my words	denken Sie an meine Worte
to market	vermarkten
May I suggest ...?	Darf ich vorschlagen ...?

May we join you?	Dürfen wir uns Ihnen anschließen?
to meet the demands	der Nachfrage entgegenkommen
to meet with a delegation	sich mit einer Delegation treffen
message	Nachricht
Ministry of Overseas Trade	Außenhandelsministerium
mobile	Mobiltelefon
multinational conference	multinationale Konferenz
name-tag	Namensschild
network	Netz (Kontakte, Straßen, etc.)
to network	Geschäftsverbindungen aufbauen
networking	Networking, Kontakte aufbauen
new entrepreneurship	neues Unternehmertum
new technology	Neue Technologie
occurrence	Vorfall
office	Büro
office manager	Office Manager
online banking	Onlinebanking
on secondment	abgeordnet sein
to open	eröffnen (ein Geschäft)
to open the conference	eine Konferenz eröffnen
opening of a conference	Konferenzeröffnung
operation	Unternehmen
to organize (a press conference, a meeting)	organisieren (eine Pressekonferenz, eine Besprechung)
overdraft	Überziehungssumme
to participate in a meeting	an einer Besprechung teilnehmen
to penetrate a market	in einen Markt vordringen
practical knowledge	praktische Erfahrung
premises	Räumlichkeiten, hier: Büroräume
to present one's business card	seine Visitenkarte zeigen
to produce new business	zu neuen Geschäften führen
professional capacity	berufliche Eigenschaft
professional freeloader	professioneller Schnorrer
profitable	Gewinn bringend
program	Programm
progressive	progressiv, fortschrittlich
promising	viel versprechend
promotion	Werbung

public share issue	Aktienemission
to put in the shade	in den Schatten stellen
to put somebody in charge of	jemandem die Verantwortung übertragen für
to put somebody through	jemanden durchstellen
to raise	etwas aufbringen
to record	aufnehmen, aufzeichnen
to register	anmelden, registrieren
reinforcement	Verstärkung
relevant papers	nötige Papiere
to represent one's company	seine Firma vertreten
to rise	steigen, ansteigen
routine	Routine
rooted in	verwurzelt mit
to run (a business)	(ein Unternehmen) leiten
to run from one appointment to another	von einer Verabredung zur nächsten rasen
sales network	Distributionsnetz
sales staff	Verkaufspersonal
schedule	Terminkalender
scupper	ruiniert
sector	Sektor, Gebiet
security in online business	Sicherheit im Online-Business
to see something through	bei etwas dabei sein
semiconductor	Halbleiter
session	Sitzung
set-up	Arbeitshintergrund
to set up a company	eine Firma gründen
shining example	leuchtendes Beispiel
to show	ausstellen
to sign for	abzeichnen, unterschreiben
slump	Wirtschaftskrise
software	Software
small change	Kleingeld
to spare	ersparen
speaker	Referent, Redner
to specialize	spezialisieren
to start with a company	bei einer Firma anfangen

to steal a march on	die Schau stehlen
stiff competition	harte Konkurrenz
strike	Streik
strong position	starke Position/Stellung
to strike somebody	jemandem auffallen
success	Erfolg
successful	erfolgreich
to switch attention	Aufmerksamkeit verlagern
tactic	Taktik, Strategie
to take a brief glance at	einen kurzen Blick werfen auf
to take a look at one's company's operation	einen Blick auf die Tätigkeiten seiner Firma werfen
to take a message	eine Nachricht entgegennehmen
to take on responsibilities	Verantwortung übernehmen
to take off	sich freinehmen
to take over	übernehmen (eine Firma, etc.)
to take place	stattfinden
team	Team, Mannschaft
timeworn	ausgedient
trade fair	Messe/Fachmesse
trade fair appearance	Messeauftritt
trade fair stand	Messestand
trait	Charakterzug
transaction	Transaktion
union	Gewerkschaft
virtual conference	virtuelle Konferenz
visitor's pass	Besucherausweis
to weaken	schwächen
to wear various hats	verschiedene Aufgaben übernehmen
well stocked	gut versorgt
What are you up to?	Woran arbeiten Sie gerade?
when it comes to	etwas betreffen
to widen the circle of contacts	den Kontaktkreis erweitern
to work for	für (etwas) arbeiten
work force	Arbeitskräfte, Mitarbeiter
working hours	Arbeitszeiten
worthwhile endeavours	lohnendes Bestreben/Bemühungen
to wrap things up	Sachen abwickeln

Solutions

Seite

7. 1. on
2. in
3. on
4. back
5. off
6. off
7. down
8. down, off
9. up
10. over

11. 1. turn it on
2. turn off
3. turn you on
4. turn out
5. turn out
6. turned over
7. out of turn
8. on the turn

13. 1. lead
2. lead
3. lead off
4. led her on
5. leading up to
6. took the lead

16. 1. had to
2. do I really have to
3. had to
4. will have to
5. had to move out
6. will have to

18. 1. certain, certainly
2. certainly, certain
3. certain
4. certain, certain
5. certainly, certain
6. certainly, certain, certainly

20. 1. did you attend
2. attend
3. attend to
4. attends to
5. attending
6. attends

22. 1. keeps on making mistakes
2. keep at it
3. keep a watch on (keep an eye on)
4. keep out of his way
5. keep your temper
6. keep each other company
7. to keep herself to herself
8. keep it secret

24. 1. in
2. up
3. up, on
4. on
5. at
6. –

27. A suggested strategy:
First of all, engage in conversation the businessperson whose company interests you. If he or she is engaged in conversation with a table companion so much the better – don't break in, but wait for an opportunity to join in, ideally by expressing your interest in your conversation partner's company. Lead the conversation into a more social, relaxed area by mentioning that your wife works for a British company, accompanying that information with complimentary

remarks about how much she enjoys working with British people! The chance meeting with the British politician who is guest of honour and your rounds of golf with the British Consul General are only of peripheral interest at functions like this. Save the business cards until the farewells - it's not normal practice to hand them out at the start of a function such as a luncheon, dinner or banquet.

29. 1. taken command
2. take (the District Line)
3. takes
4. certainly takes his time
5. taking it in turns
6. take you up on (your reasoning)
7. taken root
8. take a back seat

33. 1. it is good for
2. good for nothing
3. a good hour
4. good
5. good
6. a good number
7. split up for good
8. all for the good

36. 1. recall
2. remind
3. remember
4. recalls
5. reminds
6. remember
7. remember, remember, recalls
8. remembered

37. Turn left outside the hotel, carry straight on until you reach Lexington Avenue, again take a left turn and carry straight on until you reach 50th Street, you'll see the bar on the corner.

40. 1. left
2. leave my dog alone
3. leave us alone
4. leave to providence
5. left him with
6. leave me with
7. left
8. left

42. 1. finds out
2. find her
3. find
4. found
5. finds
6. found
7. find
8. find no cause

44. 1. not to look at it
2. Look out!
3. look after
4. looks down on them
5. look into
6. look
7. looking to
8. Look up, looking up

46. 1. somebody
2. anybody (anyone), somebody
3. no one
4. nobody (no one), somebody
5. anybody (anyone), nobody (no one)
6. somebody (someone)

48. 1. in
2. out, up on
3. out
4. off

5. through
6. on
7. up on
8. out

51. 1. your best foot forward
2. best man
3. a best face
4. best case
5. the best part of
6. best seller

53. 1. in my favour
2. in favour of
3. in its favour
4. out of favour
5. favoured
6. do me a favour

55. 1. come clean
2. come across
3. come into
4. come down through
5. come in
6. come down
7. coming along
8. come in

61. Fedorov should have said ...
This is 20 B, isn't it?
I'll move right away.
I never grow tired of looking at Moscow from the air.
Yes, I'm Russian, although I spend a lot of time in America. My two brothers are there, in business.
Oh, yes. As often as I can. And you? You are not American? To judge from your accent, you must be from Europe. Are you?
And I am Sergei Fedorov. I'm pleased to meet you.

62. 1. in the way of the traffic
2. has a way with people
3. she's well on her way.
4. was way off the mark
5. by the way,
6. he put the work away

64. 1. short
2. a short term one
3. within a very short time
4. in short order
5. short listed the candidates
6. were short sighted
7. be short lived

67. 1. make out
2. make do
3. made up
4. made light of it
5. made waves
6. make off
7. made off with
8. made public

70. 1. hands off
2. at hand
3. handed down
4. hand them in
5. handed over
6. handed down
7. at the hands of
8. on hand
9. out of hand
10. out of hand

74. 1. get on
2. get cracking
3. get after

4. got wind of
5. get a bead on
6. get a move on
7. get off
8. to get even with her

77. 1. lost, lost my heart
2. lost track
3. lose heart
4. lose his temper
5. losing time
6. lost the initiative

79. 1. that
2. this
3. that
4. this
5. that
6. that, this

83. 1. cooked to perfection
2. I'm finished, I've lost
3. exhausted
4. not acceptable

86. 1. fits and starts
2. fit to burst
3. fit in
4. fit to kill
5. fit to be tied
6. good fit
7. fitting
8. fit in

88. 1. had submitted
2. had received
3. knew
4. to be

5. had tried
6. were

91. 1. up
2. down
3. in
4. on
5. in on
6. go
7. out
8. up

95. 1. takes the cake
2. take note of
3. take stock of
4. taken heart
5. took him to task
6. took a dim view of
7. take account of
8. take charge of

97. 1. to have missed her
2. hear, have recovered
3. have caught, boarded
4. hearing, had left
5. meet, was
6. have found, am

100. 1. pick on
2. pick up
3. pick out
4. pick and choose
5. picked up
6. picked their way
7. pick up (or pick up on)
8. picked up
9. picking at
10. picked up

103. Lucy: Hello! Ergo here. Can I help you?
Caller: Thatcher of North End Electronics here. I'd like to speak to Mr Morgan please.
L. I'll see if he's free (available). Just wait (hold on, hang on) a moment, please. Mr Morgan? I have a Mr Thatcher of North End Electronics on the line. Shall I put him through?
M. No, Lucy. I'm very busy at the moment. He's calling about sales, so put him through to Steve.
L. Hello, Mr Thatcher? Mr Morgan is busy (speaking) on another line at the moment. He has asked me to put you through to Mr Blackman. Sorry to keep you waiting. I'll put you through right away. Oh dear! Mr Blackman's line is busy (engaged). Would you like to hold (hold on, hang on, wait)? His line should be free very soon.
C. No. I have a call waiting for me on another line. I'll call back.
M. Hello, Lucy? Is Thatcher still there (on the line)? I've just remembered something I wanted to discuss with him. Can you put him through?
L. No, Mr Morgan. He rang off. He says he'll call later.
M. Lucy, this is rather important. Do you think you could call his number for me?
L. Well, he said something about having a call on another line. But I'll try to reach him for you.

108. 1. must be
2. must
3. must be
4. might
5. must
6. must be
7. might be
8. must

111. 1. laid down
2. laid up
3. laid on the table
4. layabout
5. laid on
6. lay aside

7. lay
8. lay off

114. 1. I didn't think the speaker was that good. His address to the forum, in fact, was very dull.
2. He thinks he's very much an expert, but he doesn't really know that much.
3. I'm very (much) obliged to you for your assistance, which has been very far beyond the bonds of friendship.
4. She was by far the most beautiful bride I have ever seen.
5. I must say I'm rather interested in the job offer, although I can't really make up my mind.
6. Her performance of that rather difficult task was very useful to us.

116. 1. ever
2. never
3. ever
4. never, never
5. ever
6. never
7. ever
8. never

119. 1. got up
2. comes down
3. down at
4. down to
5. down on
6. having been up against

123. 1. made her mark
2. markup, on the mark
3. up to the mark
4. on their marks
5. marking time
6. lost their mark
7. marked down, lost their mark

8. markup

126. 1. has set up
2. have been, haven't had
3. has been, went
4. had, went
5. fell, visited
6. has fallen, started
7. haven't left, had set off
8. was, haven't visited

129. 1. on
2. to
3. to
4. for
5. for
6. in
7. for
8. –

Lösungen zum Abschlusstest

1. a. pleased; b. can't, relieved; c. tell, sad; d. best wishes; e. pleased, good wishes; f. excuse, taken; g. off-colour; h. propose; i. response, want; j. in, on

2. a. congratulations; b. congratulations; c. good speed!; d. good luck; e. sympathy; f. disappointment; g. concern; h. thanks

3. a. on, in; b. up, in; c. down, in; d. at, off; e. up, at; f. in, in; g. to, out; h. to, on; i. on; j. in, into